CREATIVITY

The Reality Club 4

JOHN BROCKMAN

EDITOR

A TOUCHSTONE BOOK
Published by Simon & Schuster
New York   London   Toronto   Sydney   Tokyo   Singapore

TOUCHSTONE
Simon & Schuster Building
Rockefeller Center
1230 Avenue of the Americas
New York, New York 10020

Copyright © 1993 by John Brockman Associates, Inc.
except for "Seven Creators of the Modern Era," copyright © 1993 by
Howard Gardner

Designed by Irving Perkins Associates
Manufactured in the United States of America

1 3 5 7 9 10 8 6 4 2

Library of Congress Cataloging-in-Publication Data
Creativity / John Brockman, ed.
p. cm.
"A Touchstone book."
Includes bibliographical references.
1. Creative ability. 2. Creative ability—Case studies.
I. Brockman, John, 1941–
BF408.C7533 1993
153.3′5—dc20   92-43634
                                CIP

ISBN: 0-671-78926-0

CONTENTS

QUESTIONS OF CREATIVITY

TERESA M. AMABILE AND ELIZABETH TIGHE

When I heard the learn'd astronomer,
When the proofs, the figures, were ranged in columns before me,
When I was shown the charts and diagrams, to add, divide, and
    measure them,
When I sitting heard the astronomer where he lectured with
    much applause in the lecture room,
How soon unaccountable I became tired and sick,
Till rising and gliding out I wander'd off by myself,
In the mystical moist night-air, and from time to time,
Look'd up in perfect silence at the stars.
                    —WALT WHITMAN

Art is a mystery. A mystery is something unmeasurable.
                    —E. E. CUMMINGS

We have lots of different attitudes, but in one of our attitudes as human beings, we make up a romantic tale about ourselves. Falling in love is mysterious, thinking is mysterious . . . and so we create great words like "creativity." Creativity is thinking; it just happens to be thinking that leads to results that we think are great.

Some people get very upset [at the idea that human thinking may not be mysterious]. They get upset because, somehow or other, challenging the uniqueness of human beings bothers them. . . . If you think it is terribly important that human beings should be completely different from anything else on the face of the earth, well then you probably ought to be upset.
                    —HERB SIMON[1]

THE ROMANTIC VIEW OF CREATIVITY, a view held by a good many creative persons besides Whitman and cummings, is that creativity should be left alone. Like Whitman feeling sickened by the measurement of the stars, the romantics are sickened by attempts to measure creativity. To examine it under a psychological microscope (or telescope), to ask questions of it and expect answers, is, they believe, to insult and possibly endanger it. This may be considered a psychological equivalent of the Heisenberg uncertainty principle in physics: the mere act of attempting to measure something can change the very thing we are trying to measure. Creativity, it seems, may be too fragile to withstand scrutiny.

The antiromantic view of creativity, a view held by many a hard-nosed experimental psychologist (ourselves excluded), is also that creativity should be left alone. Here, however, the reason is different. Creativity is too ill-defined a quality to be studied properly, either because it is a vacuous concept, or because it is so different from ordinary thinking that we have no tools for studying it. Moreover, the argument goes, if we define creativity as the production of the unpredictable, then it defies one of the principal aims of science: to predict.

Like Simon, we reject both arguments. For over forty years, a large number of psychologists and cognitive scientists have been actively studying creativity using, in part, the tools that have been useful in the study of ordinary cognitive processes. To be sure, much of that work has been questionable—either conceptually weak or methodologically unsound. But many of us have been asking important questions of creativity in a rigorous fashion, and we have been finding some answers. In this essay, we will present some of the questions we have been asking ourselves about creativity—questions about the nature, definition, and recognition of creativity; questions about the components of creativity; questions about influences on the creative process; and questions about the use of the creativity principles that have been discovered. It will soon become clear that we have many more questions than answers. But, we contend, each of these questions is amenable to scientific inquiry.

WHAT IS CREATIVITY?

The question of defining creativity is a knotty one. At this point in the history of inquiry into creativity, most researchers accept a conceptual definition of creativity that includes two elements: novelty and appropriateness. In order to be considered creative, a product or response must be different from what has been done before. (Few theorists hold the strong position that a creative idea must be completely *unique*.) But the product or response cannot merely be different for the sake of difference; it must also be appropriate, correct, useful, valuable, or expressive of meaning. In our own work, we add a third element. The task must have been heuristic for the individual, rather than algorithmic. That is, the task as presented must have been somehow open-ended, with no clear and straightforward path to a single solution.

IS CREATIVITY A QUALITY OF PERSONS, PROCESSES, OR PRODUCTS?

Undoubtedly, it is all three. Persons can have, in greater or lesser degrees, the ability and inclination to produce novel and appropriate work and, as such, those persons may be considered more or less creative. Processes of thought and behavior may be more or less likely to produce novel and appropriate work and, as such, those processes may be considered more or less creative. Products (scientific theories, artworks, articulated ideas, dramatic performances, and so on) may be more or less novel and appropriate and, as such, those products may be considered more or less creative. The question that concerns us as researchers is this: which approach is most amenable to scientific study?

Science is the study of observable phenomena. We contend that, ultimately, we must base a scientific study of creativity on observable products or responses. Although we may acknowledge that a highly creative person (one capable of highly creative work) can generate a highly creative thought process (one that yields highly creative ideas), that person and that thought process are not objects for scientific study unless the ideas are somehow expressed. A product can be an uttered word, a dramatic stance, a manuscript, a soufflé, a collage . . . but it must be observable by others. Hence, it is only by reference to their products (often, their accumulated products) that we can label persons as creative, and it is only by examination of the products of thought processes that we can label those processes as creative. If we base the study of creativity solely on the person, we run the risk of implying that everything done by the creative person must be creative. If we base our study solely on the process, we must be willing to define some set of distinguishing features of thought processes that will always lead to creative products, and we must be willing to assert that creative products cannot arise in the absence of those processes. At our current state of knowledge, at least, this is not possible.

HOW DO WE ASSESS CREATIVITY?

Clearly, this question is related to the last one. Many researchers have decided to focus on creativity as a quality of persons and, as a result, they have assessed creativity in terms of scores on standard creativity tests, such as Torrance's Tests of Creative Thinking or Mednick's Remote Associates Test. Because of the difficulties inherent in entering the black box, few researchers have attempted to assess creativity by the quality of thought processes—although some ingenious protocol-analysis work has been done recently.[2] Like us, some researchers have resorted to the analysis of products in the assessment of creativity. Then, when creative products have been identified, they infer creativity in the individual who produced the work, and in the individual's thought process.

But how should products be assessed? In our work, we rely on consensual assessment in our operational definition of creativity: products or responses are creative to the extent that appropriate observers agree that they are creative. In this context, appropriate observers are individuals who are familiar with a domain. For example, in studies where our subjects have produced poems, we have asked poets to serve as creativity judges. For geometrical puzzles, we have used mathematicians as judges. For collages, studio artists. The judges work independently, without influencing one another, and without being influenced by us (we do not provide them with definitions of creativity). Our assumption is that, in recognizing creativity in their domain, they know better than we do—as long as they agree in their independent judgments (and they usually do, to a surprisingly high degree). Their composite ratings are then used as our creativity measures.

The method is, of course, imperfect. It will probably not work well at the frontiers of any domain, where scientists are formulating theories that defy reality as currently understood, or where artists are turning against prior modes of expression. Moreover, if judges look only at products, they may make incorrect assumptions about the persons or the processes behind the products. Without knowledge about persons, for example, mathematician judges could not realize that a particular geometric puzzle was trivially easy (algorithmic) for an expert subject, and might therefore give the work an inflated creativity rating. And without knowledge about processes, artist judges might give a completely random product of nature a high creativity rating—if it were presented in the context of "real works." Similarly, musician judges might give a high creativity rating to a piece of computer-generated music, only to object strenuously once they discovered it had been composed by a computer. (Recall Simon's statements about the distress people feel when faced with challenges to the uniqueness of humans.)

Our original conceptual definition of creativity included three elements: novelty of response, appropriateness of response, and open-endedness of task. Each of these elements implies that there is some entity (though not necessarily a human one) to *make a response* when *faced with a task*. But we must admit that if the judged novelty and appropriateness of products are *all* that matters—in choosing aesthetic objects to admire, for example—then any product, even a random product of nature, qualifies. But if we are trying to learn something about the creative process, then there must be some deliberate process, either human or nonhuman, behind the product.

Despite limitations in the consensual assessment technique, we believe that its benefits far outweigh its costs. For one thing, *no* assessment method is useful for work that truly exceeds existing boundaries of a domain; only the test of time and historical consensus can say whether work was truly creative or merely bizarre. Moreover, the consensual assessment technique allows us to measure something as inherently unpredictable as creativity by allowing us to avoid specifying particular criteria in advance. We cannot say exactly what characteristics the next creative breakthrough in biochemistry will have, but we are confident that, in time, biochemists will reliably recognize it as such.

IS CREATIVITY A CONTINUOUS QUALITY?

Several recent theorists have stated that creativity is a discontinuous quality: the highest levels of work in the scientific, artistic, and intellectual domains of human endeavor, those widely recognized as genius level, are both quantitatively and qualitatively different from all other work done in those domains.[3] A corollary assumption that follows from this, one that is sometimes made explicit, is that the processes producing the highest levels of work are qualitatively different as well—only *they* deserve the label "creative process." We, however, believe that parsimony suggests a continuity in creative thought and work, from the lowest to the highest levels. Our expert judges have had no trouble assigning *degrees* of creativity to the work we have shown them. The processes leading to the most creative works may have drawn on levels of skill and motivation widely different from those of the least creative works, but we have no reason at the present time to believe that the processes were qualitatively different.

This argument has important implications for the methods

employed in studying creativity. If creativity is found only at the highest levels of activity in any given domain, then only those levels should be studied. Most researchers who take this approach choose their subjects on the basis of achieved eminence; the assumption is that individuals who become famous for their work in science, the arts, literature, and so on, must be truly creative. Generally, no attempt is made to assess creativity directly. Instead, eminence is assessed (by space devoted to the individual in encyclopedias, for example) or is merely assumed because the individual subject is internationally recognized (Darwin or Freud, for example). Although some researchers, such as Simonton,[4] obtain quantitative measures of the eminent individuals' lives and works, other researchers, such as Gruber,[5] rely solely on case studies where general impressions are formed about the major influences and processes in the subject's work.

Other researchers, such as ourselves, hold that creativity can and should be studied at all its levels in any domain—from its virtual absence, through low and moderate levels of "garden-variety" creativity, to the highest levels of ground-breaking creativity. Through our consensual assessment technique we obtain direct assessments of creativity along a continuum from low to high.[6] Like those who study only highly eminent individuals, we believe that people can recognize creativity when they see it. However, rather than simply relying on achieved fame as a signal of high creativity, we ask experts in the domain (say, poetry or collage-making) to rate the creativity of each of our subjects' products. Both methods rely on consensus among knowledgeable individuals, but our method explicitly asks those individuals to consider creativity in making their assessments. Our method also, of course, rests on the assumption that the processes underlying garden-variety creativity are not qualitatively different from the processes underlying ground-breaking creativity.

Surely, there appears to be a qualitative difference in *products*. The works of Picasso seem to be different in kind from the works produced by beginning art students. The theories of Einstein created new modes of thought. If there appear to be qualitative differences in products, is it possible that those products all arose from the same underlying process? As of yet, there is no clear evidence to settle the argument. But a metaphor drawn from research in dynamical systems theory may be helpful in describing how a single underlying process can lead to qualitatively different outcomes.

The system used in this metaphor is that of a horse on a treadmill; the treadmill increases its speed at a constant rate. When the treadmill begins moving slowly, the horse walks. At some point, the speed of the treadmill becomes great enough that the horse's movements become qualitatively different; the horse is now trotting. At some later point, the horse breaks into a canter and, finally, into a gallop. A quantitative change in the speed of the treadmill has produced a qualitative change in the gait pattern of the horse. An observer glancing at the horse at Time 1 (walking) would see movement that looked quite different from what she might see if she glanced at Time 3 (cantering). Each of these movement patterns looks qualitatively different, yet the underlying system in the treadmill (and in the horse) has remained the same.

We argue that it is possible, given *quantitatively* different levels of each of the components of creativity, for a single underlying process to lead to products that appear *qualitatively* different. There can be a continuity of process, whether or not there are true qualitative changes (or break points) in the creativity of products. Even if such break points exist, we believe that studying creativity at its lower levels can still illuminate the creativity of genius.

WHAT ARE THE COMPONENTS OF CREATIVITY?

In our theory of creativity, there are three basic components within the individual that are required for creativity in any domain of endeavor.[7] The first we refer to as *domain-relevant skills*. This component includes several elements relating to the individual's level of expertise (skill and potential skill) in the domain. It includes basic intelligence for doing work in the domain (often referred to as talent), knowledge acquired through formal and informal education, experience in the domain, and technical skill required. Some aspects of these skills or potential skills are innate but, of course, a great deal of development can occur through education and life experience.

The second creativity component is referred to as *creativity-relevant skills*. It includes cognitive styles and personal styles that are conducive to generating novel and useful ideas in any domain. Some creativity-relevant skills that have been identified by previous researchers include independence and non-conformity, orientation toward risk-taking, tolerance for ambiguity, perseverance, ability to break cognitive set, use of "wide categories" in storing information, and use of heuristics or techniques for generating novel ideas. To some extent, such cognitive and personal styles may be innate but it is clearly possible to develop them through education and experience.

The third creativity component is *task motivation,* one's self-perceived motivation for engaging in a particular task in a particular domain at a particular point in time. Task motivation may be primarily *intrinsic* or primarily *extrinsic*. Although both motivations frequently coexist, one is usually primary to the individual at the time of task engagement; it is this primary motivation that concerns us here. Intrinsic motivation is the motivation to engage in some activity *primarily* for its own sake—because the activity itself is involving, interesting, satisfying or personally challenging for the individual. Extrinsic motivation, by contrast, is the motivation to engage in some activity *primarily* in order to achieve some external goal, such as attaining a contracted-for reward, meeting a deadline, or winning a competition.

Task motivation, for any particular task at any particular point in time, is hypothesized to depend on two things: the individual's basic liking or disliking for tasks of this type (an underlying "trait" motivation), and the presence or absence of strong motivational cues in the social environment (leading to more temporary motivational "states"). Specifically, our research has shown that extrinsic constraints such as expected external evaluation, surveillance, contracted-for reward, competition, and restricted choice can undermine creativity by leading to higher levels of extrinsic motivation and consequently lower levels of intrinsic motivation. We have summarized these findings in the *intrinsic motivation principle of creativity:* people will be most creative when they feel motivated primarily by the interest, enjoyment, satisfaction, and challenge of the work itself (intrinsic motivators), and not by external pressures (extrinsic motivators). In other words, we propose that, in a strongly intrinsically motivated state, people will achieve the level of deep task involvement that is essential to creativity.

Recently, Sternberg and his colleagues have published a model of creativity that takes the elements in our componential model and, essentially, reorganizes those elements into somewhat different componential groupings.[8] The Sternberg–Lubart theory's knowledge component is essentially the same as our domain-relevant skills component. Their motivation component is essentially the same as our task motivation component. They divide the elements of our creativity-relevant skills component into three more elaborated components: processes of intelligence (flexibility in problem definition, reconceptualizing existing problems in new ways, and various information-processing heuristics); intellectual styles (intellectual independence, wide or global categorization of information, and risk-taking); and personality (tolerance for ambiguity, perseverance, openness to change, risk-taking, and individuality). Finally, the Sternberg–Lubart theory includes the environment as a sixth component. We, however, prefer to include as creativity components only those elements that are intraindividual, with the environment entering as a crucial influence on each individual component and on the overall process. Indeed, the environment has played a prominent role in theory building and research, particularly through our research program on social influences in task motivation and creativity.

Other recent theorists have considered the role of the environment in an even broader context.[9] These theorists suggest that the creative behavior of individuals working in a particular domain can depend heavily on the state of development of the domain itself, and on the broader social/cultural/political context in which the individual is working.

WHAT IS THE PROCESS OF CREATIVITY?

This is a question to which we currently have few answers. Many theorists, such as Herb Simon, suggest that the process underlying creative thinking is basically the same as the process underlying all intelligent acts. We share this view.

We have further developed our componential model into a speculative description of problem-solving processes, specifying the role of each of the three creativity components at each stage of the creative process.[10] We use the term "problem-solving" very broadly, to encompass activities as diverse as solving a data interpretation problem in physics and solving an aesthetic communication problem in sculpture. In our model, the first stage is problem presentation; here the individual is handed a problem to solve, or simply decides to tackle a self-identified problem. Task motivation should play an important role at this stage, because intrinsically motivated individuals are more likely to formulate problems on their own. The second stage is preparation, the gathering of necessary information and resources. Domain-relevant skills should figure prominently at this stage; if they are very strong, the preparation stage will go more quickly and smoothly than if these skills need to be built. The third stage, idea generation, depends importantly on two components: creativity-relevant skills and task motivation. The ideas generated are more likely to be creative if the individual has a high level of creative thinking skill, and if motivation is intrinsic rather than extrinsic. The fourth stage, validating the generated ideas against criteria, depends primarily on the strength of domain-relevant skills; the individual needs some knowledge of the domain in order to assess the appropriateness of the ideas. To draw once again on the horse–treadmill metaphor, the levels of the three components are analogous to the speed of the treadmill. Greater speeds (higher levels of the components) can produce gait patterns (products) that look vastly different (more creative) than those produced at lower speeds (lower levels of the components).

Because, as we have described, each of the creativity components can be influenced by the environment, the entire creative process can, of course, be influenced by the environment. But we should hesitate to call the process a "creative" one. The outcome of the problem-solving process will be deemed more or less creative to the extent that problem-finding was both unusual and accurate in Stage 1; a sufficient store of information and skill in the domain was accessed in Stage 2; at least one unusual and workable idea was generated in Stage 3; and, in Stage 4, the problem-solver was able to choose the idea that best maximized both novelty and appropriateness. If one or more of these elements are missing, either (a) no reasonable solutions (products) will be generated, or (b) technically correct but mundane solutions (products) will be generated, or (c) bizarre, unworkable solutions will be generated. For example, if an individual with a high level of domain skill and creativity skill is presented a problem in a social context of extrinsic constraint, that individual will be unlikely to fully engage those creativity skills in generating ideas. The result may be technically well done but ordinary.

WHY DO SOCIAL CONSTRAINTS INFLUENCE CREATIVITY?

As we noted earlier, our work (and the work of some other researchers) has demonstrated that social constraints such as expected evaluation and contracted-for reward can undermine creativity. Most of this work has utilized an experimental methodology: Subjects, randomly assigned to constraint or no-constraint conditions, perform identical creativity tasks (such as collage-making). The only difference is that those in the constraint condition are placed under some social-environmental constraint; they might, for example, be told to expect detailed evaluations of their work by experts. Later, the products made by all subjects are assessed on creativity by experts, using the consensual assessment technique. Our analyses of these creativity ratings have shown, fairly consistently, that creativity is lower in the presence of extrinsic constraint. Our nonexperimental studies in business organizations, primarily utilizing interviews and questionnaires with R&D scientists, have confirmed and expanded these findings.

We believe that the mechanism by which social constraint undermines creativity is a motivational one. The initial source for this belief was the demonstration of the overjustification effect in psychology. This effect, first demonstrated by researchers in the early 1970s,[11] was a startling one: rewards (and other external inducements), usually thought of as universal motivators, could actually have negative effects on motivation. Specifically, if people who were initially intrinsically interested in doing an activity were offered some external inducement for doing it, their subsequent intrinsic interest would decline. Because we find similar declines in creativity under external motivators, we speculate that intrinsic/extrinsic motivational state is the key. Furthermore, we have found evidence that higher levels of creativity are correlated with higher levels of intrinsic motivation, while lower levels of creativity are correlated with higher levels of extrinsic motivation.

HOW DOES MOTIVATIONAL STATE INFLUENCE CREATIVITY?

Although no evidence yet exists for the mechanism by which intrinsic/extrinsic motivational states might affect creativity, it may be that intrinsic motivation serves to focus attention directly on the task itself rather than on factors extraneous to the task proper. Such task-focused attention may lead to greater awareness of the details of the task itself and the complexities inherent in the task. Hence, lower levels of creativity may result from extrinsic motivation because attention is diverted from the task toward the extrinsic goal. Creativity may be greatest under intrinsic motivation because of greater task absorption and consequently greater awareness of information potentially relevant to the task.

All task engagement involves goals. Unless an individual runs out of time, becomes discouraged, or gets bored, task engagement will normally cease when a goal has been attained. Creativity may or may not be part of the goal. Task engagement might stop when a creative response has been attained or, perhaps, when a response less than creative has been attained. For tasks such as writing or painting, the ultimate goal would be to produce a creative response; for other tasks such as peg-turning, the ultimate goal might be to simply turn all of the pegs on the board. Ultimate goals will not always be attained, however. Ceasing engagement in a task prior to achievement of the ultimate goal has been referred to as "satisficing" by Simon and his colleagues.[12] Satisficing means doing the task "well enough" by simply giving a response that is satisfactory, sufficient to meet demands or requirements.

We suggest that satisficing is more likely when an individual is extrinsically motivated. This possibility might be better understood through another metaphor. In this metaphor, we begin with a presented problem; it may be writing a mathematical proof or painting a picture. Consider the problem space as a maze composed of networks of pathways that represent ways of approaching a problem solution. Exiting the maze is analogous to achieving a solution to the problem that is at least satisfactory. Different maze exploration patterns will result from different goals. If the problem-solver enters the maze for the sole purpose of attaining a reward at one of the exits, that individual will be likely to minimize time spent in the maze, finding the most straightforward, well-learned path toward an exit. Since the task is viewed merely as a means to an end, attention will be narrowed to only those paths that lead directly out of the maze toward the reward, and cognitive effort will be the minimum necessary to attain the extrinsic incentive.[13]

On the other hand, in the absence of salient extrinsic incentives, the problem-solver might explore the pathways and search for the most interesting connections that will lead to an exit (a solution). Achieving a creative response most likely requires this sort of heuristic approach to the task, exploring pathways rather than taking the well-worn, guaranteed algorithm for getting out of the maze. Individuals will most likely take the more exploratory route when they are intrinsically interested in the problem space, and when their social environment does not present salient extrinsic demands.

The point of this metaphor is that motivational state influences creativity by influencing the cognitive resources invested in a task. As Simon has suggested, motivation serves to control attention. To the extent that an extrinsic motive is *salient,* attention will be directed toward the extrinsic motive and away from the task proper. The goal of completing the task to its most creative end will be replaced with a lesser goal of doing what is necessary to achieve the subgoal induced by the presence of the extrinsic motive. This analysis of the influence of motivation on creativity, however, should not be taken to mean that intrinsic motivation *equals* high creativity, or that extrinsic motivation *equals* low creativity. Whatever leads a problem-solver to get deeply involved in thinking about the task (or exploring the maze, so to speak) will enhance creativity. Whatever draws attention away from the task, by instilling the desire to "satisfice" (or exit the maze with minimum exploration), will lessen creativity. It is possible that extremely strong levels of intrinsic motivation will not be undermined by certain extrinsic incentives; rather, in the context of strong intrinsic motivation, those incentives might only serve to deepen task involvement. For example, a scientist who is deeply passionate about her work (strongly intrinsically motivated) might only become more single-mindedly involved in that work when given recognition by the scientific community (an extrinsic motivator).

HOW CAN CREATIVITY BE DEVELOPED AND MAINTAINED IN INDIVIDUALS?

With the multitude of external constraints in our society that have been shown to inhibit creativity, the question becomes, how can we nurture creativity; how can we keep it alive? The answer, of course, is not a simple one. From peer, family, and societal interactions to genetic predispositions or innate abilities, there are an enormous number of possible influences on an individual's development. If we consider the three creativity components, however, there is evidence that each of the three may be responsive to improvement attempts. Obviously, most educational systems have been devised with the primary goal of developing domain-relevant skills. Moreover, there are several creativity-training programs designed to strengthen creativity-relevant skills. But what about intrinsic motivation? Clearly, we can make attempts to reduce the salience of extrinsic constraints in home, school, and work environments. But it will never be possible (or desirable) to completely eliminate all of the factors that might undermine intrinsic motivation. How, then, can it be maintained?

Plato makes an interesting suggestion: "[The muse] first makes man inspired, and then through these inspired ones others share in the enthusiasm, and a chain is formed, for the epic poets, all the good ones, have their excellence, not from art, but are inspired, possessed, and thus they utter all these admirable poems. So it is also with the good lyric poets."[14]

Inspiration, that state of being "possessed," is infectious. In a recent study we explored the possibility of infectious inspiration.[15] Specifically, we tried to immunize children against the negative effects of extrinsic constraints by training them to think about their work intrinsically. One group of children observed a videotape that showed two children who were "possessed" by intrinsic motivation. These two models of intrinsic motivation spoke excitedly about aspects of their schoolwork that interested them and, while acknowledging the importance of good grades and praise from parents, they firmly stated that "that's not what's really important." After viewing such models, children were then asked to describe their own intrinsic interests or ways of dealing with extrinsic constraints. In later testing sessions with a different experimenter, it was found that children who had watched the intrinsic motivation training tapes scored higher on a measure of intrinsic motivation than control group children who had watched tapes on other topics. In addition, although the control group children exhibited lower creativity when offered a reward, the trained children produced *higher* levels of creativity under contracted-for reward. The implications of this study are very exciting. Through a strengthening of intrinsic motivation—keeping attention focused on task engagement and not "settling" for attainment of subgoals—the undermining influences of common extrinsic motives can be obviated, and these motives can even be turned to serve creativity.

WHAT ARE THE ELEMENTS OF A COMPREHENSIVE THEORY OF CREATIVITY?

Understanding creativity, like understanding any aspect of human behavior, requires us to take the interactionist perspective[16]: behavior is a complex interaction between person and situation. Our componential model of creativity takes such an approach, by considering both factors within the individual and factors in the situation. Knowledge and skills relevant to the domain are primarily intrapersonal variables that will affect strategies for approaching a task and evaluating response possibilities. However, these factors are no doubt influenced by the current state of knowledge in the domain, as well as by the individual's experiences in the domain. Similarly, although thinking styles, or creativity skills, have been described as intraindividual, these are also likely affected by the situational context. For example, a person might know the creativity strategy of generating counterintuitive thoughts; however, on a job such as data coding, such creative thinking styles will probably not be engaged. Likewise, as noted earlier, we consider motivational factors to be a function of both individual interests and situational constraints. Only through consideration of the individual *and* the situation in which the creative behavior occurs can we develop a system of principles that convincingly describes the phenomenon of creativity. Our current componential model has made a start on this complex task, but much more work is necessary. Undoubtedly, the consideration of environmental influences will have to be broadened significantly beyond the conceptions of our present model. There are many ways in which the environment can interact with person factors to influence creativity: through the state of the domain, the problem space for a particular task, the development of domain-relevant skills and creativity-relevant skills, the maintenance or destruction of intrinsic motivation, and the evaluation of any particular product.

A truly interactionist model of creativity must include four features. First, there must be a continuous process of multidirectional interaction (feedback) between the individual and the situations that the individual encounters. The overjustification studies have shown that an individual's intrinsic motivation is susceptible to the situational context. In turn, we have shown that motivational changes affect creativity. A model of creativity must additionally provide for subsequent changes in the basic components of creativity as a result of performing a task creatively. Elsewhere, we have argued that the satisfying feedback obtained by completing a task creatively will no doubt affect subsequent motivation, as well as further development of domain-relevant and creativity-relevant skills.[17] Upon successful completion of a task, new knowledge acquired through task engagement will be added to the store of already existing knowledge and the creativity skills just exercised may become more habitual. A comprehensive theory of creativity must allow for such multidirectionality.

Second, the individual must be seen as an active agent, intentionally adopting goals and strategies that satisfy individual needs. Individual needs will affect the relative salience of cues provided by the situational context. For example, monetary reward will probably not affect creativity in the same way for those in desperate need of money as for those who have little need of money. A comprehensive theory of creativity must describe the role of individual characteristics in the interpretation of environmental contexts, and, indeed, in the shaping of those contexts. Our research program is taking some steps in this direction by studying stable motivational styles in individuals.

A third element that should be incorporated into a comprehensive, interactionist model of creativity is a detailed description of cognitive mechanisms. We have suggested that creativity will suffer when the individual's cognitive resources are distracted from the task at hand. Admittedly, we have little solid evidence supporting this notion. We hope to strengthen our development of creativity theory by investigating with greater scrutiny the role of cognitive factors in the creative process. For example, we are attempting to discover whether the extrinsic inducements that undermine creativity also distract attention away from the task.

Finally, the *psychological meaning* of the situation for the individual must be considered as crucial. Our research program has found that salient extrinsic inducements can change individuals' perceptions of their own motivation from intrinsic to extrinsic. However, we recognize that situation cues (such as extrinsic inducements) are not perceived equally by all. By consideration of mediating factors, such as motivational orientation, we can gain a better understanding of how extrinsic constraints might undermine creativity for some individuals, but not for others. Indeed, a comprehensive theory of creativity must consider the individual as an ever-present filter for all environmental influences.

CONCLUSION

These are a few of the creativity questions that we and other researchers are currently asking. Much remains to be discovered. The romantics might feel smugly satisfied to realize that, to a large extent, creativity remains shrouded in mystery. One might easily be overwhelmed by the apparent mystery and retreat into ignorant bliss. Bliss is pleasant, and we do not seek to make creativity unpleasant. However, we feel that the acquisition of new knowledge in any domain has greater potential to expand the domain than to stifle it. Perhaps the creative products that are brought into existence arouse a sense of mystery, but we believe that they are ultimately explainable. Gaining insight into the factors affecting creativity cannot destroy it or diminish its beauty. On the contrary, such knowledge may aid us in developing creativity and keeping it alive.

NOTES

1. Herb Simon, interview in the *Carnegie-Mellon University Magazine* (Fall 1990): 11.
2. Mihaly Csikszentmihalyi, *Beyond Boredom and Anxiety* (San Francisco: Jossey-Bass, 1975).
3. For example, see Howard Gruber, "The Evolving Systems Approach to Creative Work," *Creativity Research Journal*, 1 (1988): 27–59.
4. For example, Dean Keith Simonton, *Genius, Creativity, and Leadership* (Cambridge, MA: Harvard University Press, 1984).
5. Gruber, "Evolving Systems Approach."
6. Teresa M. Amabile, "The Social Psychology of Creativity: A Consensual Assessment Technique," *Journal of Personality and Social Psychology*, 43 (1982): 997–1013.
7. Teresa M. Amabile, *The Social Psychology of Creativity* (New York: Springer-Verlag, 1983); Teresa M. Amabile, "A Model of Creativity and Innovation in Organizations," in *Research in Organizational Behavior*, Vol. 10, edited by Barry Staw & Larry Cummings (Greenwich, CT: JAI Press, 1988); Teresa M. Amabile, "Within You, Without You: The Social Psychology of Creativity and Beyond," in *Theories of Creativity*, edited by Mark Runco & Robert Albert (Newbury Park, CA: Sage, 1990).
8. Robert Sternberg & Todd Lubart, "An Investment Theory of Creativity and Its Development," *Human Development*, 34 (1991): 1–31.
9. David Feldman, *Beyond Universals in Human Development* (Norwood, NJ: Ablex, 1980); Howard Gardner, "Creativity: An Interdisciplinary Perspective," *Creativity Research Journal*, 1

(1988): 8–26; Gruber, "Evolving Systems Approach"; Simonton, *Genius*.

10. Amabile, *Social Psychology of Creativity*, "Model of Creativity," "Within You."

11. E. Deci, "Effects of Externally Mediated Rewards on Intrinsic Motivation," *Journal of Personality and Social Psychology*, 18 (1971): 105–115.

12. Alan Newell & Herb Simon, *Human Problem Solving* (Englewood Cliffs, NJ: Prentice-Hall, 1972).

13. See Arie Kruglanski, C. Stein, & A. Ritter, "Contingencies of Exogenous Reward and Task Performance: On the 'Minimax' Principle in Instrumental Behavior," *Journal of Applied Social Psychology*, 7 (1977): 141–148.

14. Plato, *The Ion*, translated by L. Cooper, in *Plato: The Collected Dialogues*, edited by E. Hamilton and H. Cairns (New York: Pantheon Books), 218–221.

15. Beth A. Hennessey, Teresa M. Amabile, & Margaret Martinage, "Immunizing Children against the Negative Effects of Reward," *Contemporary Educational Psychology*, 14 (1989): 212–227.

16. N. Endler & D. Magnusson, "Toward an Interactional Psychology of Personality," *Psychological Bulletin*, 83 (1976): 956–974.

17. Amabile, *Social Psychology of Creativity*.

SEVEN CREATORS OF THE MODERN ERA*

HOWARD GARDNER

THE PROBLEM

I propose that seven individuals were instrumental in developing those ideas and frameworks which we consider central to the "modern era." These individuals are the British-American poet T. S. Eliot; the physicist Albert Einstein; the painter Pablo Picasso; the composer Igor Stravinsky; the dancer and choreographer Martha Graham; the political and religious leader Mahatma Gandhi; and the psychologist Sigmund Freud. There is nothing sacred about the contents of this list: I could very easily have added or substituted Virginia Woolf or V. I. Lenin or Niels Bohr. But any account of creativity in the modern era would include at least some of these individuals; if we could explain their creativity, we would have arrived at some important understanding about the creative process.

Anyone who decides to talk about creativity has at least three points (if not strikes) against him:

*This essay was first presented as a talk to the Reality Club in New York City on September 13, 1990. It has been edited only in the interest of clarity. The arguments presented here are developed much more fully in my book, tentatively entitled *Creating Minds: On the Breakthrough That Shaped Our Era*, scheduled for publication in 1993 by Basic Books.

1. Creativity is a huge and amorphous subject. Noam Chomsky calls it a mystery, rather than a problem, with the clear implication that scholars should not waste their time studying mysteries.
2. Nearly all of the work in the psychology of creativity is worth little; the track record of researchers gives little encouragement to current workers.
3. Most individuals think of themselves as being creative, and so almost any generalization is immediately arrayed against the personal experience of the audience. There is none of the respectful distance which is routinely accorded to physicists or economists who are discussing their research.

Despite these perils, I have chosen to address this subject. My plan is to comment briefly on previous approaches to the study of creativity; to introduce a new approach, which takes off from the question "Where is creativity?"; to describe a new large-scale study which I am currently undertaking; and to report some preliminary impressions from that investigation.

BIG C AND LITTLE C CREATIVITY

At the beginning I want to introduce one useful distinction: the contrast between "little C" creativity—the sort which all of us evince in our daily lives—and "big C" creativity—the kind of breakthrough which occurs only very occasionally. Each of the individuals mentioned at the beginning of this essay can be appropriately described as having realized "big C" creativity. The decision to serve salad in the middle of the meal, rather than at the beginning or end, might be considered an instance of "little C" creativity.

SOME EARLIER INVESTIGATIONS

Turning to previous psychological accounts of creativity, most of the work has been an effort to understand "little C" creativity. The most well-known work is centered around "creativity tests" which are closely modeled after intelligence tests. On a typical creativity test, one is asked how many uses one can find for a brick or a paper clip; or how many objects one can discern in a seemingly random squiggle. The more answers, and the more unique the answers, the more creative one is judged to be. These tests are highly reliable; if you do well on one, you will do well on others. But they have little if any demonstrated validity. Individuals who are creative in their work do not necessarily score better on such instruments than individuals who achieve little of a creative nature.

Willing at least to tackle "big C" questions are the psychoanalysts. Freud proposed certain personality and motivational characteristics of individuals considered to be creative in the arts and in other domains. It may well be that creative individuals are sublimating other, more "raw" desires and that they have readier access to their unconscious. But there is no proof that the presence of a certain personality trait or motivational structure makes you creative, any more so than its absence lessens the possibility that you are creative. Furthermore, the Freudian point of view does not recognize differences across domains—characteristics of creativity are thought to apply equally across diverse subject areas.

Thanks to the cognitive revolution of recent decades, psychologists are now able to deal with ideational contents and structures as well as sheer behavior. Psychologists in the cognitive tradition have devoted some attention to the processes and products of creativity. This approach focuses exclusively on what goes on *within the head* of the creative thinker—a reasonable tack for psychologists but one that proves inadequate for a rounded understanding of creativity. Attempts to simulate creativity fall short because they presuppose the selection of a proper problem as well as a determination of the data relevant to its solution—two areas which are actually central to creative activity.

TWO PROMISING APPROACHES

Recently, two more promising approaches have emerged. These are almost diametrically removed from each other—one highly quantitative, the other determinantly qualitative. But taken together, they represent the two most important lines of work currently being undertaken.

Dean Keith Simonton has performed what he calls historiometric studies. In an effort to answer questions about highly creative individuals and activities, he assembles the largest data base that he can and then performs statistical analyses on this data base. So, for instance, he can discern whether individuals who work in different domains achieve their most important work during different decades of their lives; or whether individuals who are more creative maintain a different relationship to their mentors than those who are less creative. The art in this research comes in determining which data bases are relevant to answering such long-standing questions. The limitation comes in understanding the fine structure of particular creative thoughts or products.

Complementing the quantitative approach of Simonton are the efforts of the developmental psychologist Howard Gruber. A student of Piaget, Gruber has been carrying out intensive case studies of highly creative individuals in the sciences, such as Charles Darwin and Piaget himself. He details the period during which such individuals arrived at their most important ideas. In the process he has discerned some characteristics which tend to permeate the lives and works of such individuals: a wide-scale "network of enterprise"; a fondness for images of wide scope; a strong and abiding sense of purpose. The art in Gruber's work comes in attempting to capture the cognitive, affective, and personality states of the creative individual at his most critical moments. The limitation centers on the extent to which findings obtained with one individual emerge as applicable to other creative individuals as well. I believe that a happy conjunction of these two approaches would provide a tremendous boost for creativity studies.

A PRELIMINARY DEFINITION

I begin with a definition of the individual creative person. On this definition, which has emerged as a result of collaborative work with David Feldman and Mihaly Csikszentmihalyi, a creative individual is one who regularly solves problems, fashions products, and/or poses new questions in a domain in a way which is initially considered novel but which is ultimately accepted in at least one cultural setting.

This definition merits unpacking, particularly with respect to the ways in which it differs from earlier formulations. A first point has to do with regularity. Creative individuals are rarely if ever "flashes-in-the-pan": they exhibit a style of living and thinking which leads to a regularity of breakthroughs, most minor, a few of epochal importance. A second and crucial point is that creativity occurs in domains. That is, a creative individual is never creative across the board. Rather, creative individuals display their creativity in disciplines or crafts; usually in one domain, though occasionally, as in the case of Leonardo da Vinci, in two or even three domains. Note, however, that even Leonardo—the Renaissance genius par excellence—was hardly creative in every domain. Neither his music nor his poetry nor his relationships with other individuals are particularly noteworthy.

That creative individuals solve problems is not controversial. Indeed, most definitions restrict creativity to problem-solving, often gerrymandering behaviors in a quite extraordinary way so that they can qualify as examples of problem-solving. Quite frequently, however, creative individuals are notable less for the problems that they solve than for the products which they fashion—ranging from heroic symphonies to educated students—or for the new questions which they raise (for example,

Einstein's famous query about what a light beam would look like to someone traveling at the speed of light, or John Cage's attempts to incorporate chance elements into the musical composition process).

Nearly everyone who defines creativity notes that creative behaviors are initially novel or original but that ultimately they become accepted. If they are not initially novel, no one would consider them creative. And if they are not ultimately accepted, then they may be bizarre or anomalous but not creative.

However, my definition takes a further, more controversial turn. On this definition no person or work or process can be considered creative unless it is so deemed by relevant social institutions. Following Csikszentmihalyi I term this social dimension "the field." The social institutions or fields will vary enormously from one domain to another. Thus in the case of a domain like physics, the relevant field can be as small as a dozen knowledgeable peers; in painting, it is a mélange of critics, gallery owners, agents, and the art-loving public; while in newspaper or magazine publishing, the field can consist of thousands or millions of purchasers. The field may operate quickly or slowly; be steadfast in its judgments or highly fickle; but in the end the field must issue judgments about creativity, because no other set of standards can be invoked. Absent some consensus within a relevant field, the most one can say about a putatively creative individual or product is that "one can't tell."

Here, then, is a provisional definition of creativity, framed in terms of the individual. Note that, *mutatis mutandis,* this definition can easily be reworded so that it applies to a creative product (one judged as such by the field) or process (a biological, psychological, or sociological process that leads to a judgment of creativity).

A RESEARCH PROGRAM

Armed with this provisional definition, it is possible to lay out a program of research. As I initially formulated it some years ago, the study of creativity is inherently an interdisciplinary undertaking. Indeed, to elucidate creative persons or products, one should take into account four distinct disciplinary perspectives:

1. *The subpersonal.* Here one analyzes the creative individual in terms of neurobiological factors, particularly those of genetics, neurophysiology, and neuropsychology. So far there is little to say about creativity from the subpersonal or neurobiological perspective. But techniques already exist whereby it is possible to study the neurology of creativity *in vivo.* Surely such investigation will come to pass soon enough and so the subpersonal perspective deserves a place in any interdisciplinary study of creativity.

2. *The personal.* Roughly speaking, this spans the psychological level. Studies of creative individuals certainly should focus on cognitive aspects—the particular intellectual strengths and proclivities of the individual. Equally relevant are aspects of personality, motivation, will, and other noncognitive or less cognitive features of the human person.

3. *The impersonal.* An important part of the creative configuration is the nature of the domain in which an individual works. Adapting a term of David Feldman's, "domain" is used here as an umbrella term to cover academic disciplines as well as arts, crafts, and other pursuits which feature performances or productions of various degrees of expertise. So long as there exists structure of knowledge and/or of performances which can be so specified that a novice can acquire expertise, it seems legitimate to talk of a domain. I use the term "impersonal" here to stress the point that, at least in theory, knowledge of the domain could be contained in a nonliving entity, such as a textbook. In practice, however, most individuals come to know, and to master, a domain by virtue of an intensive apprenticeship with other individuals.

4. *The multipersonal.* As a complement to the impersonal domain, there exists the relevant field, a complex of individuals and institutions which pass judgment on the various products in a domain. Just as one must study the nature of the discipline or craft in which the creative individual works, so, too, it is important to understand the operations of the "judgment-making bodies" within and across domains. One might say that impersonal domain study smacks of epistemology, while the multipersonal field study relies most heavily on sociology.

Following the recipe of interdisciplinary study, then, a "synthetic-scientific approach" to creativity involves at least these four disciplinary perspectives. In earlier writings, I applied this framework to the lives and works of Sigmund Freud and Pablo Picasso; I propose now to bring it to bear on the lives and works of several creative individuals who lived around the turn of the century.

WHERE IS CREATIVITY?

I believe that the study of creativity was significantly enhanced a few years ago when Mihaly Csikszentmihalyi proposed that researchers asking "What is creativity?" or "Who is creative?" instead tackle the question "Where is creativity?" Csikszentmihalyi proposed that creativity lies not at a single locus but rather in the dynamic interaction among three nodes: the individual person or talent; the formal structure of knowledge in a domain; and the institutional gatekeeping mechanism, or field.

The scheme can be concretized by the following example. Say that there are one thousand budding painters at work in New York City, each with his or her peculiar strengths and styles. All of these individuals attempt some mastery of the domain of painting, as it now exists; and all of them address their work, sooner or later, to the field—the set of gallery owners, art school departments, newspaper critics, agents, and the like. Of these individuals, a few will be selected as worthy of special attention by the field; and at least today, their novelty will be a significant factor in their selection. Of these individuals, at most one or two will paint in a manner which becomes so esteemed that their efforts will ultimately have some effect on the domain—on the structure of knowledge which must be mastered by the next generation of painters. We can see here that creativity lies not in the head of the artist (or in his hand), not in the domain of practices, or in the set of judges; rather, the phenomenon of creativity can only—or at least, best—be understood by taking into account the interaction among these three nodes.

Painting, however, may seem an idiosyncratic domain, perhaps one where the field assumes undue importance. What of a contrasting domain, such as mathematics? I submit that the processes here are essentially the same. Substitute for our thousand artists an equal number of mathematicians, say topologists. Each of these students must master the domain the best they can and those who want to move on must address their proofs and their discoveries to the field—this time a set of professors, journal editors, prize givers. Only a few of the young topologists will stand out in terms of professorships and publications; and of these even fewer will actually affect the domain in which they work sufficiently so that the next generation of youthful topologists will encounter an altered domain.

The field is as important in mathematics as in the visual arts. It differs chiefly in that it is somewhat smaller and far more consensual in its judgments. (By an amusing coincidence, the mathematics community awards every four years a medal to the most gifted mathematician under the age of forty, called the Field Medal!)

In my view the Csikszentmihalyi triad of person, domain, and field provides the critical skeleton for an enriched understanding of creative individuals and products. Recently, in an effort to put flesh on this skeleton, I have begun a study of highly creative individuals. This study has helped me to understand some of the ways in which a careful examination of each of the three nodes, and the relations which obtain among them, can enhance our understanding of creativity. In what follows I briefly describe my study. I then indicate some of my preliminary findings, as they have emerged from a fleshed-out version of the Csikszentmihalyi skeletal triangle.

THE STUDY

Between the years of 1880 and 1930 major revolutions occurred in a number of domains, ranging from politics to science to the arts. Considered jointly, they are often termed the advent of modernism or the modern era. Reflecting the range of human talents or intelligences, as noted earlier I have been studying the creative breakthroughs associated with T. S. Eliot, Albert Einstein, Pablo Picasso, Igor Stravinsky, Martha Graham, Mahatma Gandhi, and Sigmund Freud. In carrying out this study I seek to illuminate their individual creativities, discovering those features which seem to cut across domains and persons, and those which seem restricted to particular individuals. At the same time I hope that I may be able to say something of significance about the modern era.

As previously mentioned, I could have selected different individuals—Virginia Woolf or James Joyce instead of Eliot; Lenin or Mao Zedong rather than Gandhi—there is nothing sacred or sacrosanct about my list. My goal, however, was not to anoint the seven *most* creative individuals, but simply to select seven individuals of uncontroversially creative status.

Some are uncomfortable with an exercise which places a few individuals on a pedestal. Why not study people who came close but did not make it, or more ordinary individuals? Certainly my study is not an attempt to claim that one should not study the French psychologist Pierre Janet, in his day as well known as Freud; or Freud's friend Wilhelm Fliess, to whom Freud deferred during the period of his breakthrough but who turns out to have been a crackpot. Yet, again, by focusing on individuals who are considered both creative and successful, I think one is more likely to shed light on general issues of creative productivity.

By design, my study of each of these individuals focuses on

them as persons, on the domains in which they worked, and on the operation of the fields which policed their domains. I hope that my study conveys a deeper grasp of each of these three nodes as well as a better understanding of the relations among them. Specifically, I claim that there are certain areas of "action" in each of these nodes as well as certain habitual "tensions." Studies should, I submit, focus on these areas of "action" and "tension." My study has also suggested some features which seem to differentiate these individuals from one another, as well as other properties which have cut across the individuals studied so far. Finally, the study has indicated some developmental considerations—elements to look out for at the ontogenetic and at the microgenetic level.

THE PERSON

Turning first to the node of the individual person, I detect two major areas of action. The first has to do with the relationships among the individual's intelligences. Creative individuals are characterized not only by outstanding intelligences (Picasso's spatial capacities, Einstein's logical-mathematical abilities) but also by unusual configurations of intelligence (Freud's very strong linguistic and personal understandings are unusual in a scientist; Picasso's weak scholastic abilities probably reinforced his total dedication to life as a painter).

The second area of action within the person has to do with the nature of intimate relationships at the time of a creative breakthrough. Creative individuals tend to be very independent and are often quite happy to be isolates. At the time of their greatest breakthroughs, however, they characteristically need to have an intimate to whom they can confide their thoughts. Whether it is Freud with Fliess, Picasso with Georges Braque, Eliot with Ezra Pound, or Graham with Louis Horst, these vulnerable individuals gain affective as well as intellectual sustenance from an alter ego.

THE DOMAIN

Turning next to the node of the domain, there are again two areas of action. The first has to do with how highly structured the domain is. Academic physics and academic painting are highly structured, in the sense that there exist many levels en route to expertise and these are well delineated and agreed upon by experts. Contemporary painting, creation of computer software, and good city management are far less well-structured domains.

A second and related aspect concerns the extent to which there exists a single dominant paradigm within the domain, as opposed to two or more manifestly competing paradigms. Physics after Newton had one dominant paradigm, but in the years before Einstein, a number of less well-entrenched paradigms competed for attention. During the height of classical music, the classical sonata form became the norm; two centuries later, Stravinsky's chromatic and polytonal styles competed with Schönberg's atonal, serial style.

THE FIELD

There are two areas of action at the field node. One has to do with the size of the relevant field and, in particular, the degree of hierarchy. The number of physicists at Einstein's time was small, and of that number, the opinions of Hendrik Lorentz, Jules-Henri Poincaré, and Max Planck were so important that they alone could determine the reputation of a worker. The second factor pertains to the degree of consensus which obtains within the domain. In certain fields at certain times the field is characterized by wide consensus, while at other times it is sharply divided. Thus the same field which wholly embraced Stravinsky's "Firebird Suite" in 1910 was sharply divided about "Le Sacre du Printemps," initially performed just three years later.

Now it might be thought that domain and field simply mirror each other, and indeed there is a strong connection between this pair of nodes. A tightly structured domain is more likely to have a hierarchically arranged field; and a domain with one dominant paradigm is more likely to have consensual judgments. Yet the two dimensions can and should be kept separate. At certain times a loosely structured domain (like rock and roll) may achieve a high degree of consensus (that is, regarding the merit of the Beatles); by the same token a domain with a single dominant paradigm may exhibit little consensus, as in the case of contemporary judgments of Mozart's compositions.

TENSIONS ACROSS NODES

My study suggests that creativity is particularly likely to occur when a degree of tension exists between or across the three nodes. I have already suggested some of the tensions that may occur within nodes—for instance, within a set of intelligences or between two paradigms in a domain. But perhaps more compelling are the tensions which emerge across the nodes.

Consider, for instance, the disjunction between a person and a domain. Freud's profile of intelligences was highly unusual for a scientist. Most scientists are strongest in logical–mathematical and spatial intelligences but Freud stood out for his linguistic and personal knowledge. While he was a competent neurologist and neuroanatomist, his abilities did not mesh strongly with his initially chosen domain. One he began to study clinical psychiatry, his abilities fell into closer synchrony with the demands of the domain. Still, until he founded psychoanalysis, he was never really well synchronized with the domains (and the fields) where he was working.

Picasso presents the example of an individual in tension with a field. In this instance, the young and prodigious Picasso was appreciated by family and friends; and after a difficult start as a young Spaniard attempting to survive in Paris, he had begun to attract an audience and patrons as well. But Picasso deliberately turned his back on the realistic portrayals of the blue and rose periods and began to paint in a harsh and nonrepresentational way, thus inducing a strong tension between himself and the field. Ultimately, of course, his cubist works came to be accepted—if not loved—and Picasso's highly creative output was appreciated by an ever-widening field.

It is possible to envision a tension or asynchrony between a domain and a field. In the early decades of the century, classical music veered in two directions: the harsh, rhythmic, polytonal music of Stravinsky, and the calculatedly atonal twelve-tone music of Schönberg. At the time it was by no means clear which of these two directions would ultimately prevail and, at various times, the field (or the fields) tilted in one direction or another; even Stravinsky composed in the twelve-tone style. Now it appears that twelve-tone music no longer exercises much of a hold on the musical world; one might say that the field has voted against serial music, while remaining more sympathetic to the option embraced by Stravinsky.

DEVELOPMENTAL PERSPECTIVE

While not offering a formula for the understanding of creativity, the analysis in terms of "points of action" and "asynchronies" within domain, field, and talent does give one powerful leverage for an investigation of the creative process. One might think of these categories as a set of lenses through which one may peer at any candidate creative individual, product, or process. In this context it is important to maintain a developmental perspective, for the relations between and among the three nodes are likely to change significantly over the course of an individual's working life.

During the early years of development, particularly in areas where there are prodigies, one can anticipate a strong link between talents and domains; indeed, as David Feldman has demonstrated, a prodigy is defined by a strong fit. Eventually, however, a point will come when a discrepancy or asynchrony arises—between the individual and the domain, the individual and the field, or in some other internodal arena. Sometimes, as in the case of Freud, the asynchrony seems to be intrinsic; in other cases, as with Picasso, the asynchrony may well be instigated by the individual himself, as a means of "raising the ante."

My investigations suggest discernible developmental patterns, at both the ontogenetic and the microgenetic level. Looking at the broader pattern of an individual's development, the first ten years emerge as the time when the individual attains the mastery of the domain as currently practiced. In the case of prodigies, this mastery occurs very early—by the time they were teenagers, Mozart and Picasso had already achieved the level of their masters. The crucial decade can occur much later, however: Van Gogh did not hit his stride until his thirties; Gandhi, Freud, and their followers operated in domains where mastery is unlikely to come about until middle age.

In the case of the modern masters, there tends to be a strongly iconoclastic work about a decade or so after they have begun to work in earnest in their domain. It is often this "breakaway" or "breakthrough work" which first attracts attention, sometimes positively, sometimes more controversially. Candidates for this position would be Stravinsky's "Rite of Spring," Picasso's *Les Demoiselles d'Avignon,* Eliot's "Prufrock," Einstein's special theory of relativity, Freud's Project for a Scientific Psychology. Then, approximately a decade later, there is another radical work, this one, however, more general and more comprehensive, and more likely to exhibit integral connections to the rest of the domain. This latter work has something of the Final Statement about it. These more comprehensive works would include Stravinsky's "Les Noces," Picasso's *Three Musicians* or *Guernica,* Eliot's *Wasteland,* Freud's *Interpretation of Dreams,* and of course Einstein's general theory of relativity.

One can see the asynchrony working at close hand when one studies the individual at the time of his or her major breakthrough. At least in those areas where individuals are conducting conceptual investigations, a set of steps like the following can be discerned:

1. The individual works in an unproblematic way in his or her domain—business as usual.
2. A discrepant element emerges. The individual attempts to deal with this discrepant element by conducting some kind of local surgery. However, the discrepant element keeps reemerging and is not easily eliminated.
3. The discrepant element "spreads" and "works." The individual finds that the discrepant element, far from being an error or nuisance, actually provides an important and generative element to his or her inquiries. The individual seeks to understand the once-discrepant but now generative element in depth and to develop a symbol system with which to work on the element.
4. Having established to his or her satisfaction that the once-discrepant element is a powerful and generative one, the individual now seeks to share these insights with a broader field. This step involves the invention of a new symbolic form which can communicate with a wider audience; it often entails miscommunication, feedback, and revision, as the individual and others attempt to test the system's limits and to promulgate the new formulation.
5. Finally, the system works sufficiently well and powerfully so that it takes on a life of its own. To some extent this is a positive development since the particular perspective of the discoverer is no longer all-determining. However, not infrequently, the system becomes redirected and perverted, as the domain and field move in unpredictable and uncontrollable ways.

As developed so far, this scheme seems to be a reasonable description of what occurs in such concept-rich domains as science (physics) and clinical studies (psychoanalysis). Whether it can be adapted appropriately for use as well with performances like dance, or with social institutions like a nonviolent protest, remains to be determined.

DIFFERENCES AND SIMILARITIES

My studies have also suggested a number of differences and similarities which can be discerned across the several creative individuals whom I have been studying. Turning first to the differences, I note several:

1. *Need/inclination to campaign for oneself.* Some discoverers, like Einstein, have shown little tendency to promote themselves or their works, preferring to leave this mission to others. Others, like Freud, have been tireless promoters of their apparent achievements.

2. *Relations to rivals.* Einstein showed little interest in his rivals and was able to maintain reasonable relationships with almost all of them. Stravinsky and Picasso were far more embattled, having little good to say about anyone else.

3. *Need for close confidants.* Nearly all of the creative individuals benefited from the reactions and support of an alter ego during the time of their maximum isolation. But at other times, these creative individuals differed widely from one another in terms of the amount of support which they needed or desired. Also, in some cases (such as Freud), the support came primarily from individuals of the same sex, whereas in other cases (such as Picasso), the support was rooted chiefly in a relationship with someone of the opposite sex.

4. *Role of collaboration.* In some cases—for example, poets or painters—collaboration is a luxury which need not be indulged in. Others, however, have careers in which collaboration is of the essence. Thus a composer of theatrical works, like Stravinsky, and the designer of a new social movement, like Gandhi, are involved on a daily basis in complex interactions with other individuals.

5. *Role of prodigiousness.* As already noted, prodigiousness is common or even expected in certain domains, such as mathematics or music. In others, however, it is rare (painting) or even unknown (clinical medicine).

6. *Ability to be creative within a given domain.* Some workers, like Picasso and Einstein, make their greatest breakthroughs in domains which have already been quite well defined. Others, however, like Gandhi and Freud, are better thought of as inventing a new domain, or perhaps radically restructuring one or more domains that had already existed.

It is possible to point to a set of similarities among the creative individuals, not all of them expected:

1. *Combination of childlike and mature.* All of the creative individuals have advanced to a sophisticated and mature level in at least one domain in their culture. At the same time, however, they manage to retain a childlike quality, which enables them to pose questions in a naive way, to see things afresh, to transgress customary boundaries. They also appear in many ways to be like an amalgam of child and adult. Possibly one reason that breakthroughs occur in early life is that it is more difficult to sustain such neoteny as the years pass.

2. *Long-term trend from the world to the self and back to the world again.* As young children, these future creators are amazingly open to the experiences of the world and seem to take things in an almost effortless way. They are like sponges, to whom nothing in the world is foreign. Still, at the time of their breakthrough, they often seem to be quite sealed off, almost entirely alone. But then, following the working through of their fundamental insight or reorientation, they once again seek to make contact with the wider world, and to locate their discovery in many contexts.

3. *The inclination to be daring and bold.* Without such audacity, and the ability to withstand criticism, it is unlikely that they could have persevered and prevailed. Interestingly, nearly all of them comment that they have little sympathy for—and even

little understanding of—an individual who would be nondaring, who would be content with the conventional.

    4. *A certain degree of marginality.* All of my sample set were in some way or another marginal in their chosen domain—through place of birth, gender, religion, or some combination thereof. Perhaps more important, they felt marginal from an early age and continued to feel marginal even when, to others, these creators were taken to be members of the relevant establishment in their field.

SUMMARY

I assert that, so far, psychology and other social sciences have provided little illumination about human creative processes and persons at their creative heights. Possible clues for a more adequate study of creativity come from the quantitative approach of Dean Keith Simonton and the qualitative studies of Howard Gruber. And perhaps the crucial insight for investigations comes from the reconceptualization by Mihaly Csikszentmihalyi, who directs us to ask the question "Where is creativity?"

Building on Csikszentmihalyi's formulation, I have taken a closer look at the three nodes of his triangle. I have defined certain "points of action" within the nodes of person, domain, and field. And I have sought to identify recurring kinds of tensions or asynchronies which emerge within and especially across these three nodes. It is here that I find the greatest insight into the emerging phenomena of creativity.

My inquiry thus far has suggested that these asynchronies can be observed both ontogenetically, in the trajectory from apprentice to master and from the revolutionary to the synthesizer, and microgenetically, at the time when the discovery of greatest moment has been made. In the process I have also identified several features which seem to differentiate among the masters, as well as another cluster of features which so far are exemplified by all of them.

Of course, it remains a task for the future to determine

whether these generalizations will hold across other creative individuals, other domains, and other times. My study does suggest one characterization of the modern era: it is a time when individuals have been able to unite some of the questions and understandings of earliest childhood—the first years of life—with the tools and understandings acquired in sophisticated mastery of a domain. Whether it is Einstein asking about traveling on a beam of light, Freud following his dreams and free associations, Gandhi achieving a goal in light of lesser physical strength, or Graham using the most elemental gestures to convey fear, hope, or triumph, all of our modern masters are at once children and sages. I doubt that one would find the same union of the toddler and the titan in other eras; but perhaps breakthroughs in other eras or epochs relate mastery to other, later stages of human childhood.

READING LIST

Csikszentmihalyi, M. (1988). "Society, Culture, and Person: A Systems View of Creativity," in *The Nature of Creativity*, edited by R. J. Sternberg (New York: Cambridge University Press), pp. 325–339.

Feldman, D. H. (1980). *Beyond Universals in Cognitive Development* (Norwood, NJ: Ablex).

Gardner, H. (1982). *Art, Mind, and Brain: A Cognitive Approach to Creativity* (New York: Basic Books).

Gardner, H. (in press). *Creating Minds: On the Breakthroughs That Shaped Our Era* (New York: Basic Books).

Gruber, H. (1981). *Darwin on Man* (Chicago: University of Chicago Press).

Simonton, D. K. (1984). *Genius, Creativity, and Leadership* (Cambridge, MA: Harvard University Press).

ASPECTS OF SCIENTIFIC DISCOVERY: AESTHETICS AND COGNITION*

Howard E. Gruber

SOMETIME IN THE mid-1970s a new alliance developed among various disciplines that have something to say about the many aspects of a knowing system. These disciplines included cognitive psychology, neurology, artificial intelligence, philosophy of science, linguistics, and part of anthropology. In a short time "cognitive science," as the alliance called itself, had journals, professional meetings, and training programs. Since almost anything about an organism has some connection with knowing, we need to ask, What is *not* cognitive science? A recent encyclopedic (2.2-kg) volume, *Foundations of Cognitive Science* (Posner, 1989), is revealing. Omitted or given very

*A version of this essay was presented at a conference on scientific discovery in the biomedical field at the Royal Society of Medicine in London, October 1989. Another version appeared in a volume edited by R. M. Downs, L. S. Liben, and D. S. Palermo, *Visions of Aesthetics, the Environment and Development: The Legacy of Joachim F. Wohwill* (Hillsdale, NJ: Erlbaum, 1991). I thank Margery Franklin and Doris Wallace for their valuable suggestions.

short shrift are developmental psychology, creativity, history, motivation, and emotion. This is a digitalized, decontextualized dry kind of knowing. What is not "computational" doesn't exist.

The term "computational" doesn't necessarily mean that something can really be computed—it is enough that one can envision an approach that might lead to computing it someday. "Envision"?? What's that? Vision, too, gets short shrift in cognitive science. Even perception is only included under the banner "A computational study of vision." As might be expected, since development is excluded, play does not appear either. The reader may well ask, How can anything be discovered without play, perception, and vision?

After a description of "antiseptic" cognitive science similar to mine as just given, Howard Gardner sums up:

> Some critics [of cognitivism] hold that factors like affect, history, or context will *never* be explicable by science: they are inherently humanistic or aesthetic dimensions. . . . Since these factors are central to human experience, any science that attempts to exclude them is doomed from the start. Other critics [argue that] cognitive scientists should from the first put their noses to the grindstone and incorporate such dimensions fully into their models. (Gardner, 1985, p. 42)

This situation puts people interested in scientific creativity in a position requiring choice. We can accept the sterilization required by cognitive science as it is now practiced, or we can strike out in whatever directions necessary to capture scientific discovery as it takes place in a complex, historically and culturally conditioned world, a world that is by no means "antiseptic."

A cognitive-science approach to scientific discovery can be expected to portray the production of a series of problem-solving efforts, a sequence of theoretical models or belief systems, and a series of real-world encounters in which new facts are assimilated into changing mental structures.

But if we want to situate the process of scientific discovery within the context of a purposeful creative *life,* we need another approach, one that includes the cognitive sciences as they have styled themselves but persistently transgresses the limits they have set. Indeed, the cognitive sciences most concerned—cognitive psychology and philosophy of science—have no conceptual apparatus and no method for dealing with a creative life. A similar point can as well be made not only about scientific discovery, but also about the study of other kinds of creativity. The milieu within which individual cognition and cognitive development take place is not only the external objective and social contexts rightly emphasized by sociological and ecological thinkers. There is also the *internal milieu* that includes the whole gamut of emotions, motives, values, and aesthetic feelings.

The present essay is an attempt to transgress one of the boundaries set by mainstream cognitive science, to study the relation between aesthetics and cognition. This effort is part of a larger program in which my collaborators and I have devoted our energies to the use of the case study method, to try to reconstruct pictures of real creative people at work (Gruber, 1985; Vidal, 1989; and Wallace & Gruber, 1989). Peculiarly enough, we think we are cognitive scientists too!

We labor under a special difficulty, unknown to investigators who are only interested in characteristics and processes shared by all human beings, or for that matter, all knowing systems: each creator is necessarily unique, and it is his or her uniqueness above all that we would like to understand. This is the inescapable task of the student of creative lives. Still, a few common characteristics emerge, providing at least general guidelines for studying the unique creative person. I make this concession a little reluctantly, for all too often the identification of these common features is taken as the end of the inquiry rather than what it should be—only the beginning of the study of creative work.

THE ORGANIZATION OF PURPOSE

One of these common points is the simple finding that creative work, being difficult, generally takes a long time. This prolonged activity requires a powerful organization of purpose to maintain it. Typically, the work of the creator is organized into what we have called a "network of enterprise." Although the subjects I have focused on—Charles Darwin and Jean Piaget, among others—have had wide and diversified networks, there is as yet no special theoretical reason to insist that the creator's network of enterprise must be both wide and diverse.

In examining various networks of enterprise I have found that they often go dormant as a natural consequence of the multiple preoccupations of vigorous but, after all, finite beings. But they rarely die out completely.

The question now arises, What motivates the creative person? To some extent we can say that the network of enterprise has motivating power: tasks undertaken become their own justification, the felt need to complete them the spur. Intrinsic motivation and task orientation (Lewin, 1935; Amabile, 1983) as opposed to ego orientation, the instinct of workmanship (Veblen, 1914), functional autonomy (Allport, 1937)—these are all terms that have been used to capture this aspect of the motivation of work.

The creator is probably not entirely aware of his or her network of enterprise—not aware, that is, of all its strands and interconnections. Nevertheless, it is close enough to consciousness that it serves the creator's purposes as a valuable organizing tool for making decisions about what to do next and for managing the interruptions that are a well-nigh inevitable concomitant of the pursuit of a difficult task carried out in the real world.

THE ORGANIZATION OF AFFECT AND AESTHETIC EXPERIENCE

But this organization of purpose must be linked with an organization of affect, or emotion. Just what are the satisfactions and frustrations to which the creator responds? How does it feel when the going is good?—or bad? Psychologists interested in emotion chronically focus attention on negative affects— anxiety, depression, fear, guilt, anger, hate. Without denying the power of these darker forces, we must also ask, What are the positive feelings that reward the creative person at work, the presence and prospect of which draw him or her ever back into the unfinished work, and on and on through the long struggle?

The principal aim of this essay is to address one aspect of that question. More specifically, I want to focus attention on aesthetic feelings that arise in a life devoted to science. And here I feel most timid, on thin ice. While there is a wealth of philosophical writing on aesthetics, it is not easy to move into the aesthetics of science.

Of course, to the working scientist it is not news that scientific work provokes moments of great feelings of beauty and awe, or other aesthetic experiences. When scientists write or talk about their lives, they often tell about such moments. So our task is to get beyond the mere bow of recognition to aesthetics in science to something more probing and in the long run more systematic. For this we will look at a few cases in some detail—especially Charles Darwin and Jean Piaget. But first I want to touch on a few general questions. This essay is frankly an exploratory effort, and I do not hope to answer all the questions I raise.

ASPECTS OF THE AESTHETIC EXPERIENCE
IN SCIENCE

First, we should take cognizance of the point of view reflected when we speak of aesthetic *feelings,* such as feelings of beauty and awe. Aestheticians are divided on this matter, but for understanding scientific discovery it seems to me that the right place to locate aesthetic experience is as one region within the affective domain, a region where cognition and emotion interact.

Second, it seems to me that the appropriate unit of analysis is not a single emotion or feeling, such as might occupy a few seconds, but rather an emotional experience, a structured period of time, set off from other such experiences. Metaphorically, we are not speaking of single notes or chords, but rather of phrases, movements, and sonatas.

Third, in this enlarged idea of an emotional experience, it may be that any feeling might participate. Scratchiness prepares the way for smoothness, calm for thunder, frustration or sadness for joy, banality for astonishment. This prompts the question, If any feeling can participate, what makes an experience an aesthetic one?

Fourth, how does the shape of aesthetic experience change during the life history of the creative person?

Fifth, what are the connections between the organization of affect and the other great organizations—knowledge and purpose—at work in a creative life?

Sixth, to what extent does the creative person have control over the occurrence and course of emotional experiences? Are emotions merely reactions *to* events in the creative life, or are they also purposeful acts and part of the process?

Seventh, what is the actual function of aesthetic experience in the process of scientific discovery? Psychologists interested in emotion have traditionally differed as to whether its function is primarily expressive, energetic, or directive. My impression is that scientists writing about their own lives often emphasize the directive function, as in statements insisting on the ultimate truth value of beautiful theories, even when the latter seem to be contradicted by the facts currently available. Sometimes, then, the desire to make one's science more aesthetically satisfying actually guides the direction of the work (see Hoffmann, 1990; Levi-Montalcini, 1988; Piaget, 1976; and Yukawa, 1982).

Finally, can science be taught well without adequate attention being given to aesthetic experience in science? *Inter alia,* is the approach that says "first learn enough, then you'll appreciate it" self-defeating?

VARIETIES OF AESTHETIC EXPERIENCE

When we ask more specifically, "What is aesthetic experience?" a useful way to begin is by trying to separate characteristics of the experiencing subject from properties of the object (or process, or idea) contemplated. When we say, "Beauty is in the eye of the beholder," we implicitly take cognizance of this distinction, for the statement suggests its corollary, that beauty is *not* in the object. Feelings of beauty and awe are good examples of subjective experience, while attributes of symmetry and complexity are examples of properties of objects.

In addition to properties of objects and experiences of subjects, a third aspect of aesthetic experience in scientific discovery must be the form or medium in which it is represented, both to the experiencing subject and to the world. Images, metaphors, diagrams, narratives, raw feelings—all these and others come to mind as media in which aesthetic experiences take shape. I mention this here for completeness but will not discuss it further.

AESTHETIC MOOD

I believe it is safe to say that the aesthetic of simplicity, symmetry, and harmony has been the dominant mood among those discussing the aesthetics of science. (See, for example, *Fearful Symmetry: The Search for Beauty in Modern Physics* [A.

Zee, 1986]. Likewise, C. N. Yang's "Beauty and Theoretical Physics" [1980].) But an aesthetic of asymmetry, complexity, and diversity has found contemporary voices. For example, in his essay "On Broken Symmetries," the physicist Philip Morrison writes:

> What we regard as highly satisfying works of art, even many natural things of beauty, contain broken symmetries. The symmetry is made manifest in some form, yet it is not carried out to perfection. The contrast, making visible both sides of the act of becoming, demands appreciation. (Morrison, 1978, p. 70)

Freeman Dyson's essay "Manchester and Athens," in *The Aesthetic Dimension of Science* (Dyson, 1980), and my own paper "Darwin's 'Tree of Nature' and Other Images of Wide Scope," in *On Aesthetics in Science* (Gruber, 1978), also discuss the aesthetics of asymmetry, complexity, and diversity.

In the second half of our century a third aesthetic has come into prominence, the aesthetic of the absurd, the incoherent, the quasi-formless. Beckett's *Waiting for Godot* and Pollock's paintings come to mind as examples, and in science, more recently, the "chaos" movement (Gleick, 1987). A Nobel laureate in physics, the late Richard Feynman, gave voice to a measure of acceptance of this mood:

> The theory of quantum electrodynamics describes Nature as absurd from the point of view of common sense. And it agrees fully with experiment. So I hope you can accept Nature as She is—absurd.
>
> I'm going to have fun telling you about this absurdity, because I find it delightful. (Feynman, 1985)

A physicist I spoke with about the aesthetic of the absurd objected that "chaos" is not absurd, but refers to definite, comprehensible physical processes. Maybe so, but they are absurd enough to have merited the name "chaos."

Rather than casting the discussion in the framework of a di-

or trichotomy between two or three aesthetics, there is another approach that takes fuller account of the diversity of aesthetic experiences. Each person may exhibit particular forms of aesthetic experience, and by attending to the many aspects of this domain we may be able, eventually, to draw a multidimensional profile of each person and each experience. This approach would also help us to describe developmental changes over the life history. E. F. Keller, in her biography of the Nobel laureate geneticist Barbara McClintock, has given a good picture of someone whose unusual aesthetic profile led her to her major discoveries (Keller, 1983).

For the present I will simply list two sets of attributes of aesthetic experience, one for the experiencing subject and one for the contemplated object, as discussed earlier. These lists are provisional and incomplete, based on a number of conversations, and on autobiographical and other accounts written by scientists. In some cases I have specified both members of a pair of polar opposites and listed them together; I have also listed near-synonyms together. In all cases these are not terms drawn from a thesaurus but descriptions actually given by people experiencing scientific discovery, and talking or writing about it in a mood of interest in the aesthetic experience.

For the contemplated object
Order, pattern, rhythm, repetition, regularity
Modularity (and nonmodularity)
Universality
Law, inevitability
Uniqueness
Simplicity, unity, harmony
Fitness, correspondence, invariance
Balance, equilibrium, symmetry (and broken symmetry)
Complexity, diversity, intricacy
Density, richness of nature
Growth, progress
Reversibility, irreversibility

For the experiencing subject

Awe

Beauty, admiration of nature, of science

Surprise, astonishment

Joy, ecstasy, elation

Struggle

Pleasure of contemplation, fascination

Strangeness, familiarity

Expansiveness, flow, growth

With regard to each potential attribute of the aesthetic experience, there is probably no absolute value that is decisive. It is, rather, change in awareness that evokes the aesthetic experience. In our thinking about these matters, however, room must somehow be made for repeated changes: a symphony does not lose its value or its freshness at the second hearing. Csikszentmihalyi's concept of "flow"—happy, exultant response to challenge—is a sensitive attempt to take account of this need for continuous extension of the self through cycles of strenuous effort, mastery, and accomplishment (Csikszentmihalyi & Csikszentmihalyi, 1988).

The importance of each attribute to the creator cannot be measured by a frequency count of the number of times he or she mentions it. For example, one cannot imagine D'Arcy Thompson's great work, *On Growth and Form*, without imagining the writer as someone in love with pattern; and one cannot appreciate the book without sharing this love. Yet it is written in a rather dry style, and only in the epilogue at the end of the second volume does the author drop the veil:

For the harmony of the world is made manifest in Form and Number, and the heart and soul and all the poetry of Natural Philosophy are embodied in the concept of mathematical beauty. (Thompson, 1917/1942, Vol. 2, pp. 1096–1097)

I turn now to the examination in some detail of one scientist's aesthetic experience.

CHARLES DARWIN'S AESTHETIC FATE

My mind seems to have become a kind of machine for grinding
general laws out of large collections of facts, but why this should
have caused the atrophy of that part of the brain alone, on which
the higher tastes depend, I cannot conceive. . . . The loss of these
tastes is a loss of happiness, and may possibly be injurious to
the intellect, and more probably to the moral character, by en-
feebling the emotional part of our nature. (Charles Darwin,
Autobiography, 1958 [posthumous], p. 139)

Darwin's well-known confession of the atrophy of his aesthetic
sensibilities should be taken seriously, but taken in context.
To do this we must look at the trajectory of Darwin's aesthetic
development. He wrote his *Autobiography* between the ages of
sixty-seven and seventy-three. In it he describes his earlier
interest in various arts—music, poetry, fiction, drama, painting. From this document, from his notebooks, and from his
published writings, it has been possible to reconstruct a fairly
full account of Darwin's aesthetic tastes and development in
the arts. (For a recent and probing effort, see Gillian Beer's
Darwin's Plots [1983]). It appears that Darwin had a long and
very full period of interest in the arts, fluctuating in intensity
from moderate to very strong. Even in his later years he retained a love of fiction, especially novels with happy endings,
as might befit an apostle of evolutionary progress.

More to the point, perhaps, is an examination of Darwin's
scientific work. Line for line, he was not an especially eloquent
writer. For literary style he certainly could not match his colleague, Thomas Huxley. The power of his writing, his ability
to evoke the reader's aesthetic feelings, lies more in the structure and fullness of his argument, and in his devoted, tireless
marshaling of the evidence to support it. Still, we often see,
especially in the closing paragraphs of his chapters, a sudden
turn toward a more eloquent and passionate style. As I have
already pointed out in the case of D'Arcy Thompson, it is
reasonable to suppose that Darwin's feelings thus overtly ex-

pressed from time to time, and in strategic places, actually suffused his whole work.

There is, furthermore, no reason to suppose that there was some mysterious split between the aesthetic feelings Darwin evoked in others and those he felt himself. It is much more plausible that he felt the feelings he evoked. This idea, that he was a vicarious reader of his own writings, may apply even to the feelings of outrage he provoked in his antagonists. Darwin could empathize with them, and this enabled him to use various literary devices either to defang or to placate his critics, as well as to answer them directly.

A key passage in Darwin's writings is the closing paragraph of the *Origin of Species,* the celebrated "tangled bank" metaphor. Here is clearly expressed Darwin's synthesis of the two aesthetics, simplicity and complexity. On the one hand he evokes the richness of nature; on the other hand, he extols the few laws that, taken together, can explain this richness.

It is interesting to contemplate an entangled bank, clothed with many plants of many kinds, with birds singing on the bushes, with various insects flitting about, and with worms crawling through the damp earth, and to reflect that these elaborately constructed forms, so different from each other, and dependent on each other in so complex a manner, have all been produced by laws acting around us. These laws, taken in the largest sense, being Growth with Reproduction; Inheritance which is almost implied by reproduction; Variability from the indirect and direct action of the external conditions of life, and from use and disuse; a Ratio of Increase so high as to lead to a Struggle for Life, and as a consequence of Natural Selection, entailing Divergence of Character and the Extinction of less-improved forms. Thus, from the war of nature, from famine and death, the most exalted object which we are capable of conceiving, namely, the production of the higher animals directly follows. There is grandeur in this view of life, with its several powers, having been originally breathed into a few forms or into one; and that, whilst this planet has gone cycling on according to the fixed law of gravity, from so simple a beginning endless forms most beau-

tiful and most wonderful have been, and are being, evolved.
(Darwin, 1859)

We encounter a similar, albeit less developed, duality in Darwin's vision in a passage in the *Beagle Diary,* the more personal notes he kept during his voyage, alongside of the scientific notes.

I believe from what I have seen Humboldt's glorious descriptions are & will for ever be unparalleled: but even he with his dark blue skies & the rare union of poetry with science which he so strongly displays when writing on tropical scenery, with all this falls far short of the truth. The delight one experiences in such times bewilders the mind: if the eye attempts to follow the flight of a gaudy butter-fly, it is arrested by some strange tree or fruit; if watching an insect one forgets it in the stranger flower it is crawling over; if turning to admire the splendour of the scenery, the individual character of the foreground fixes the attention. The mind is a chaos of delight out of which a world of further & more quiet pleasure will arise. I am at present fit only to read Humboldt; he like another sun illumines everything I behold. (*Beagle Diary,* p. 39, written Feb. 28, 1832, when Darwin was twenty-three years old, on first visiting Bahia, Brazil)

For Dawin, this was a momentous occasion, akin to one of Wordsworth's "spots of time," as shown in a remark about the same scene, written the next day:

To a person fond of natural history, such a day as this brings with it pleasure more acute than he may ever again experience. (*Beagle Diary,* p. 40, Feb. 29, 1832)

On revisiting this scene later in the voyage, Darwin's diary entry displayed the same dualism, the same movement of ideas between wildness and taming:

. . . the land is one great wild, untidy luxuriant hot house, which nature made for her menageries, but man has taken possession of it, & has studded it with gay houses and formal gardens. (*Beagle Diary,* p. 417, Aug. 1–6, 1836)

A quarter of a century later, in the concluding passage of the *Origin of Species,* Darwin displayed the same dualism. But now the focus is not the contrast betwen the subject-oriented "chaos of delight" and "quiet pleasure," or between the object-oriented "wild, untidy luxuriant" nature and "formal gardens." Now the epistemological movement is between the visible "entangled bank" and the inferred "laws acting around us." When Darwin wrote "There is grandeur in this view of life," he was writing neither of the wildness nor of the laws, but of the productive relations between them. (See *Origin of Species* [1859/1966], pp. 489–490.)

Various writers have mentioned Darwin's love of Milton's poetry, the fact that it was the one book he carried everywhere during the voyage of the *Beagle,* and the Miltonic voice in which he often wrote. Gillian Beer has pointed out some pertinent passages in Milton's *Comus:*

> Wherefore did Nature pour her bounties forth.
> With such a full and unwithdrawing hand.
> Covering the earth with odors, fruits, and flocks.
> Thronging the seas with spawn innumerable,
> But all to please, and sate the curious taste? . . .

Milton goes on to argue that man must consume immensely, to counteract this superfecundity of nature, otherwise:

> . . . strangled with her waste fertility,
> Th'earth cumbered, and the winged air darkened with plumes;
> The herds would over-multitude their lords.
> (*Comus,* lines 710–714 and 728–731, cited in Beer, 1983, p. 35)

To this I would only add that it seems plausible to me that Darwin read the highly erotic, rhymed verse of his grandfather, Erasmus Darwin, while still an adolescent in Shrewsbury. In both poets the richness of the world was a powerful theme. Milton was the greater poet, but Erasmus Darwin was closer to home. He was also easier to read and a good bridge to Milton. Elsewhere (Gruber, 1981; Keegan & Gruber, 1983),

I have discussed the relevant proto-Malthusian—and now we see, Miltonic—passages in Erasmus Darwin's poetry, such as this one, which has quite a Miltonic ring:

All these, increasing by successive birth,
Would each o'er people ocean, air and earth . . .
The births and deaths contend with equal strife,
And every pore of Nature teems with Life.
(Erasmus Darwin, *Temple of Nature,* 1803 [posthumous], canto IV)

I have said enough to recall the poetic origins and echoes to be found in Charles Darwin's thinking. But in addition to the particular passages I have cited, or others that might be cited with similar import, there is a more general point—the simple fact that Darwin had the occasion to write the *Beagle Diary* and later the *Journal of Researches* (1839) as a free-ranging account of the voyage of the *Beagle.* The latter work is not simply a travel book enlivened with descriptive natural history. It is a great travel book, and it is that because it is permeated with Darwin's burgeoning theoretical preoccupations during and immediately after the voyage. (See Gruber, *Darwin on Man,* 1981, Appendix: "The Many Voyages of the *Beagle.*")

I believe that creative workers often find some form in which to elaborate an *initial sketch* of important works to follow, sometimes much later. Westfall (1980) has described this process for Isaac Newton, my student Tahir (1989) has done the same for George Bernard Shaw, and I will report later on a similar stage in the work of Jean Piaget. For creative scientists, the use of a relatively free literary form may be one good way to get some ideas said provisionally, unhampered by the demands of scientific discipline.

I return now to the celebrated case of atrophy of aesthetic sensibility recounted in Darwin's *Autobiography.* Somewhat paradoxically, first I discuss possible reasons for it, then I question its extent and generality.

We can probably not attribute the change in Darwin to a general loss of gusto sometimes associated with aging; Darwin claims that the change began twenty to thirty years earlier, in other words, when he was in his forties or younger, or before he wrote his greatest works. Nor can it have been that an overwhelming preoccupation with work excluded all distractions and amusements. We know he had time to listen to readings of novels, and he had time for his children and friends, and for various community activities.

What, then? It seems to me that cultural life, especially in the countryside of Down, may not have been all that stimulating. Moreover, the time in question was the heyday of the Victorian age. Perhaps Darwin did not come across any new material that would have captured and reawakened his attention at any time in his life. As for rereading Shakespeare and Wordsworth, he had already done that. Sometime, probably in the 1840s, he had read Wordsworth's *The Excursion* twice. Since he never left Britain after the voyage, the scenery he saw in later years was all more or less familiar to him, and therefore lacking the aesthetic impact of surprise.

Finally, he did not entirely lose his touch as an imaginative writer. The ingenuity of his late botanical experiments and of his studies of the behavior of earthworms excites our admiration. And, true to form, the closing passage of his last work, finished in 1882, the year of his death, displays the same sense of paradox, the same antinomic cast as we have encountered in his earlier writings. This time the paradox is not between wild and tame, or entanglement and law, but between the lowly and the mighty, minute cause and great effect:

When we behold a wide, turf-covered expanse, we should remember that its smoothness, on which so much of its beauty depends, is mainly due to all the inequalities having been slowly levelled by worms. It is a marvellous reflection that the whole of the superficial mould over any such expanse has passed, and will again pass, every few years through the bodies of worms. The plough is one of the most ancient and most valuable of man's inventions; but long before he existed the land was in fact regularly ploughed, and still continues to be thus ploughed by earth-worms. (Darwin, 1882, *The Formation of Vegetable Mould Through the Action of Worms, With Observations on Their Habits*)

It is worth noting the consistency with which Darwin used this antinomic literary device. *The Descent of Man* (1871) closes with a passage having a similar structure, this time declaring the contrast between humanity's lowly origins and the "godlike" creatures we have become.

I do not introduce all these qualifications of Darwin's autobiographical remarks on aesthetic atrophy in order to deny their importance. But seen in their life history context those remarks do not seriously challenge the idea that aesthetic sensibility is a ubiquitous and indispensable part of the process of scientific discovery.

JEAN PIAGET'S SENSE OF MISSION

Jean Piaget, the great Swiss psychologist and epistemologist, provides a sharp contrast to Darwin. At the age of nineteen he published a long prose poem, *La Mission de l'Idée,* in which he expressed his burgeoning ideas about religion, science, and philosophy (Piaget, 1915; see also Gruber, 1982). By that time he was already an established malacologist, with over twenty published articles, some of them lengthy monographs, to his credit. A few years later he published a philosophical novel, *Recherche* (Piaget, 1918), which includes a very interesting initial sketch of what was to become his life work. In spite of these literary beginnings, Piaget's later writings are notorious for their turgidity and opacity. Which only shows how important it is to study the whole person, for he was a clear, witty, and brilliant lecturer.

From Piaget's early writings one might have predicted his development toward a humanist, philosophical style, similar to Henri Bergson, whom he greatly admired. But he moved in the direction of increasing formalism in his attempt to logicize child thought. We can find his gusto and sense of play in the techniques he and his collaborators used to bring out children's thinking. But this disappears very quickly in Piaget's insistent formalism. We know, or guess, that the poet is still there, but he is hidden under a mass of symbols that are hard to appreciate, much less understand.

At the same time, Piaget maintained a lifelong interest in literature and music. He loved Proust and Bach. And he never lost his interest and pleasure in the world of nature—both the Alpine scenery that surrounded him in his walks and his child-like yet sophisticated pleasure in finding interesting specimens of snails, or of the plant genus *Sedum,* which he studied and wrote about for many years.

In a seminal work, *Icon and Idea: The Function of Art in the Development of Human Consciousness,* Herbert Read (1955) took up the theme of the necessity of aesthetic experience for the well-functioning of mind: "Poetry is a taking possession of reality, a first establishment of the frontiers of reality in our understanding" (Read, 1955, p. 18). He cites Heidegger:

> Poetry is the establishment of being by means of the word . . . poetry is the inaugural meaning given to being . . . not just any speech, but that particular kind which for the first time brings into . . . consciousness . . . the essence of all things—all that we can then discuss and deal with in everyday language. (Quoted in Read, 1955, p. 18)

The creator, especially when starting out—as part of the process of commitment to a line of work, to a first and fateful set of projects, and to a personal style—needs some rich and flexible medium in which to explore the broad range of possibilities. Private notebooks can play this role, as Holmes (1989) has shown for Lavoisier, Bernard, and Krebs. Darwin, too, used his notebooks to this end, but, as I have shown (Gruber, 1981), he also used his great travel book about the *Beagle* voyage as a medium for exploring issues in the theoretical biology prevalent in his youth. Perhaps we ought to speak of "poetic liberty" rather than poetic license.

Part of this poetic liberty of the creator starting out is the search for an appropriate medium. And the medium appropriate for first moves is often abandoned along the way. The young Piaget had some sense of this, for he wrote:

The poet feels in himself a higher beauty, that his verses cannot paint and that they half kill. In his soul he attends a sorcerer's symphony of virtualities, a procession of dreams, colored and alive. But reality is singular, expresses only one of these possibilities, even depriving him of that which makes his true life. (Piaget, 1915, verse VI, p. 10, translated by H. E. Gruber for this essay)

In a beautiful chapter on adolescent thinking, Inhelder and Piaget (1955) have discussed the adolescent's discovery of the set of all possible things and of the romantic, newly egocentric upsurge of exploratory, utopian, and even oceanic thinking that is liberated then, as a prelude to the productive work to follow.

Perhaps this chapter has something quite autobiographical in it. Its tone and its content, perhaps alone among Piaget's later works, remind one of his youthful prose poem, *La Mission de l'Idée*. In Piaget's later work on the "equilibration model" of development (1985), he elaborates the theme that development takes the path of successive equilibrations and disequilibrations, leading to ever higher and more powerful forms of thought. He spoke of this as "équilibration majorante," which has been translated as "optimizing equilibration." Perhaps it would be better to say "reoptimizing," since the optimum does not stand still. In any event, the fundamental thought form is to consider that the way out of each cognitive developmental impasse is to move upward on the ladder of abstraction.

It is fascinating to discover this metaphor of *moving upward* in various passages in the prose poem, *Mission*. In one verse of the sixty-eight-page work he creates an image of two boys lost in the forest:

The one worshipped, then persuaded himself that reality was good and the trails of the forest were a wise work whose unknown laws would not let him get lost. In his sincere faith he departed, refusing to look at anything but the end that his faith saw. He abdicated because he was afraid, and made himself stupid because he mistrusted himself.

The other doubted, thought. Then only did he pray. He felt the good in reality, but because he was courageous and because truth was dearer to him than his own happiness, he climbed a tree and studied the depths of the forest. And thus through his search he spied a pathway. He took heart and rushed toward it joyously.

Such is faith and such is sincere doubt. What the first boy calls humility is often only fear and cowardice. What the second calls scepticism is often only respect for an ideal of truth. (Piaget, 1915, verse XXXIII, p. 50, translated by H. E. Gruber for this essay)

The same theme of upward movement reappears in the final verse of *Mission:*

. . . When the idea is reborn, every man now suffering in the shadows will find his place in the vast harmony which by its crescendo will make life grow, so high that it will see God. But the rebirth of the idea requires the help of everyone. Metaphysics is not an aristocratic art. The scientist, who finds hypotheses, must build over them a grand edifice that can contain them; the Christian, who in the depths of his heart has felt a life, must assimilate it by an interpretation which justifies it; the moral man, who wants a rule of conduct to govern his life, must construct an idea to justify it. The special mark of each man must be his idea and from these ideals, numerous as the cells, the true idea will come forth like the soul from the body.

Oh! that the tears shed during the war bear this beautiful fruit: the new birth of Christianity.

For that is the mission of the Idea.

(Piaget, 1915, verse XLVI, p. 67, translated by H. E. Gruber & J. J. Vonèche in Gruber & Vonèche, 1977)

In my illustrations chosen from the lives of Darwin and Piaget for this essay, I have chosen to emphasize one major theme for each: Darwin's recurrent interest in the antinomy between order and complexity, captured in his image of the "tangled bank"; Piaget's enthrallment with the strategy of always transcending the level thus far achieved, captured in his telling phrase "équilbration majorante."

But I do not mean to suggest that each creative life can be reduced to one major theme. On the contrary, it is the interweaving of a number of themes and thought forms that makes up the fabric of a creator's thought.* To distinguish the stable ideas from those emerging and those declining requires the careful study of the subject's whole oeuvre.

DIFFERENT STROKES FOR DIFFERENT FOLKS

DIVERSITY

In looking at the lives of various creative scientists it becomes apparent that the aesthetic dimensions of their lives are quite varied. Consider two examples.

Salvador Luria, the biologist, Nobel laureate himself and mentor of James Watson of *Double Helix* fame, in his autobiography (1984), mentions only briefly certain moments of ecstasy in his scientific work. Although he does not in this work make much of the aesthetic side of his scientific life, he devotes a whole chapter to his protracted struggles to develop his extrascientific tastes, his appreciation of various arts. His efforts and pleasures in this vein continued unabated into his seventies.

Robert B. Woodward, the organic chemist, must have been one of the most single-minded scientists of his time. His daughter, Crystal Woodward, has written a biographical account (Woodward, 1989). She makes him appear almost monomaniacal in his pursuit of organic synthesis, in his immersion in his laboratory, and in his painstaking and brilliant visualizations of organic chemical structures. In her account he seems to have had little extrascientific aesthetic life, except for his personal style—dressed always in blue—and his beautiful, polished lectures, which he illustrated at the chalkboard, always with his personal set of colored chalks. His Nobel Prize citation mentioned specifically his contributions to "the art of

---

*I have developed this idea in more detail in other writings (Gruber, 1978, 1981; Gruber & Davis, 1988).

organic synthesis." And his private notes show a constant attention to drawing skill and pleasure on the occasion of discovery. A colleague, Frank Westheimer, wrote of him:

> Even scientists who mastered his methods could not match his style. For there is an elegance about Woodward's work—his chemistry, his lectures, his publications—that was natural to him, and as unique as the product itself.
>
> His real style was most clearly expressed in the syntheses themselves, in the ways he found to put molecules together, ways that somehow feel right—each step neatly designed to prepare for the next, a kind of art that combined inevitability with surprise, as in great classical music. (Cited in Woodward, 1989)

DIVERSITY IN SIMILARITY

In the annals of science there is hardly a more striking coincidence than the independent invention of the theory of evolution through natural selection by two men, Charles Darwin and Alfred Russel Wallace. Even when the creative product of two creators' efforts is quite similar, as with Darwin and Wallace, there is good reason to believe that the aesthetic trajectory of their lives is not. Darwin and Wallace, for all the similarity of the contents of their thought during one crucial period, differed widely in personal and scientific style; they also took quite different directions in their later works. Darwin's autobiography is short and quietly witty, Wallace's long and sincere.

Perhaps the most dramatic example of this diversity in similarity is provided by the lives of Picasso and Braque. For a time they collaborated closely in the creation of cubism, and their individual works were virtually indistinguishable. But even at their closest there were important differences. Not only did they have different personal styles, but the overall development of their life histories was very different. I believe that when we make similar comparisons of scientists we will find the same diversity in similarity.

THE FUNCTIONS OF AESTHETIC EXPERIENCE

Given our knowledge of the diversity of aesthetic experience, both in style and in developmental pattern, there is no reason to expect to find the same profile of functions for all creative scientists, or to presuppose that each form the aesthetic impulse takes in any one scientist has the same function. The physicist Richard Feynman took drawing lessons regularly for many years. He was also a talented and enthusiastic drummer. His lectures in physics were noted for their elegance, wit, and clarity. Although, toward the end of his life, Feynman wrote two humorous autobiographical books, his writing was not especially introspective. If we must guess, we probably would not guess that all these various expressions of his aesthetic feelings grew out of a single motive force. Rather, they are the workings of a many-sided mind.

The idea of a profile of functions may be useful here. We can identify various functions that play some part in aesthetic experiences and activities, and we can devise means of indicating the relative importance of each function in a particular creator's life. The functions I have in mind include the following: expressive and decorative, recreational, motivational, and constitutive. The constitutive functions of aesthetic experience are themselves complex since they include the idea of initial sketch, the suggestion and discovery of novelty, and the synthesis or integration of ideas and observations into more powerful, better organized schemata. Even one form of aesthetic expression, such as metaphor, may have all these functions. But to grasp the significance of a particular aesthetic act we must know the creator's life and work, and know them well.

I have been using almost interchangeably such terms as "aesthetic experience" and "aesthetic act." I think this is justified, because the purpose of such acts is to engender such experiences, and the experiences cannot occur without the acts.

Eleanor Duckworth (1987) called her book about science education *The Having of Wonderful Ideas*. For a creative scientist there is no lure, no motive power more powerful than the prospect of having some of those. That feeling of wondrousness is both the rainbow and the rainbow's end. To draw students into the web of scientific work scientists should find ways to let their students know that this rainbow is their destination.

READING LIST

Allport, G. W. (1937). "The Functional Autonomy of Motives," *American Journal of Psychology*, 50: 141–156.

Amabile, T. (1983). *The Social Psychology of Creativity* (New York: Springer Verlag).

Beer, G. (1983). *Darwin's Plots: Evolutionary Narrative in Darwin, George Eliot and Nineteenth Century Fiction* (London: Rutledge & Kegan Paul).

Csikszentmihalyi, M., & Csikszentmihalyi, I. (1988). *Optimal Experience: Psychological Studies of Flow in Consciousness* (Cambridge: The University Press).

Darwin, C. R. (1839). *Journal of Researches into the Geology and Natural History of the Various Countries Visited by H.M.S. Beagle under the Command of Captain FitzRoy, R.N. from 1832 to 1836.* (London: Colburn, 1839; 2d edition, London: Murray, 1845).

Darwin, C. (1859). *On the Origin of Species* (London: Murray).

Darwin, C. (1871). *The Descent of Man and Selection in Relation to Sex* (London: Murray).

Darwin, C. (1882). *The Formation of Vegetable Mould Through the Action of Worms, With Observations on Their Habits* (London: Murray).

Darwin, C. (1934, posthumous). *Charles Darwin's Diary of the Voyage of H.M.S. "Beagle,"* edited from the manuscript by Nora Barlow (Cambridge: The University Press).

Darwin, C. (1958, posthumous). *The Autobiography of Charles Darwin (1809–1882),* edited by his granddaughter, Nora Barlow (London: Collins).

Darwin, E. (1803, posthumous). *The Temple of Nature; or the Origin of Society* (London: Johnson).

Duckworth, E. (1987). *The Having of Wonderful Ideas and Other Essays on Teaching and Learning* (New York: Teachers College Press).

Dyson, F. (1980). "Manchester and Athens," in *The Aesthetic Di-*

mension of Science, edited by D. W. Curtin (New York: Philosophical Library), pp. 41–62.

Feynman, R. P. (1985). *QED: The Strange Theory of Light and Matter* (Princeton, NJ: Princeton University Press).

Feynman, R. P. (1985). *"Surely You're Joking, Mr. Feynman!"* (New York: W. W. Norton).

Feynman, R. P. (1988). *"What Do You Care What Other People Think?"* (New York: W. W. Norton).

Gardner, H. (1985). *The Mind's New Science: A History of the Cognitive Revolution* (New York: Basic Books).

Gleick, J. (1987). *Chaos: Making a New Science* (New York: Penguin).

Gruber, H. E. (1978). "Darwin's 'Tree of Nature' and Other Images of Wide Scope," in *On Aesthetics in Science,* edited by J. Wechsler (Cambridge, MA: MIT Press), pp. 121–142.

Gruber, H. E. (1981). *Darwin on Man: A Psychological Study of Scientific Creativity,* 2nd ed. (Chicago: University of Chicago Press; original work published 1974). See especially the appendix to the 2nd edition, "The Many Voyages of the *Beagle.*"

Gruber, H. E. (1982). "Piaget's Mission," *Social Research,* 49:239–264.

Gruber, H. E. (1985). "Going the Limit: Toward the Construction of Darwin's Theory (1832–1839)," in *The Darwinian Heritage,* edited by D. Kohn (Princeton: Princeton University Press), pp. 9–34.

Gruber, H. E., & Davis, S. N. (1988). "Inching Our Way Up Mount Olympus: The Evolving Systems Approach to Creativity," in *The Nature of Creativity,* edited by R. J. Sternberg (New York: Cambridge University Press).

Gruber, H. E., & Vonèche, J. J. (1977). *The Essential Piaget* (New York: Basic Books).

Hoffmann, R. (1990). "Molecular Beauty," *Journal of Aesthetics and Art Criticism,* 48:192–204.

Holmes, F. L. (1974). *Claude Bernard and Animal Chemistry.* (Cambrdige, MA: Harvard University Press).

Holmes, F. L. (1989). "Antoine Lavoisier and Hans Krebs: Two Styles of Scientific Creativity," in *Creative People at Work: Twelve Cognitive Case Studies,* edited by D. B. Wallace & H. E. Gruber (New York: Oxford University Press).

Inhelder, B., & Piaget, J. (1955). *The Growth of Logical Thinking: From Childhood to Adolescence* (New York: Basic Books).

Keegan, R. T., & Gruber, H. E. (1983). "Love, Death, and Continuity in Darwin's Thinking," *Journal of the History of the Behavioral Sciences,* 19:15–30.

Keller, E. F. (1983). *A Feeling for the Organism* (San Francisco: Freeman).

Levi-Montalcini, R. (1988). *In Praise of Imperfection: My Life and Work* (New York: Basic Books).

Lewin, K. (1935). *A Dynamic Theory of Personality* (New York: McGraw-Hill).

Luria, S. E. (1984). *A Slot Machine, A Broken Test Tube: An Autobiography* (New York: Harper & Row).

Morrison, P. (1978). "On Broken Symmetries," in *On Aesthetics in Science,* edited by J. Wechsler (Cambridge, MA: MIT Press), pp. 55–72.

Piaget, J. (1915). *La Mission de l'Idée* (Lausanne: la Concorde), 68 pp. A partial translation exists in H. E. Gruber & J. J. Vonèche, *The Essential Piaget* (New York: Basic Books, 1977), pp. 26–41.

Piaget, J. (1918). *Recherche* (Lausanne: la Concorde), 210 pp.

Piaget, J. (1976). "Autobiographie," *Revue européene des sciences sociales,* 14:1–43. An incomplete English version exists in the series *History of Psychology in Autobiography* (Worcester, MA: Clark University Press, 1952), pp. 237–256.

Piaget, J. (1985). *The Equilibration of Cognitive Structures: The Central Problem of Development.* (Chicago: University of Chicago Press) (Original work published 1975).

Posner, M. I. (Ed.) (1989). *Foundations of Cognitive Science* (Cambridge, MA: MIT Press).

Read, H. (1955). *Icon and Idea: The Function of Art in the Development of Human Consciousness* (Cambridge, MA: Harvard University Press).

Tahir, L. (1989). "The Development of Thought in Young Bernard Shaw," unpublished doctoral dissertation, Rutgers University, Newark, NJ.

Thompson, D'Arcy (1942). *On Growth and Form,* 2nd ed., 2 vols. (Cambridge: University Press). (Original work published 1917.)

Veblen, T. (1914). *The Instinct of Workmanship and the State of the Industrial Arts* (New York: Macmillan).

Vidal, F. (1989). "Self and Oeuvre in Jean Piaget's Youth," in *Creative People at Work: Twelve Cognitive Case Studies,* edited by D. B. Wallace & H. E. Gruber (New York: Oxford University Press).

Wallace, D. B., & Gruber, H. E. (1989). *Creative People at Work:*

Twelve Cognitive Case Studies (New York: Oxford University Press).

Westfall, R. S. (1980). "Newton's Marvelous Years of Discovery and Their Aftermath: Myth versus Manuscripts," *Isis,* 71:109–121.

Woodward, C. E. (1989). "Art and Elegance in the Synthesis of Organic Compounds: Robert Burns Woodward," in *Creative People at Work: Twelve Cognitive Case Studies,* edited by D. B. Wallace & H. E. Gruber (New York: Oxford University Press), pp. 227–253.

Yang, C. N. (1980). "Beauty and Theoretical Physics," in *The Aesthetic Dimension of Science,* edited by D. W. Curtin (New York: Philosophical Library), pp. 25–40.

Yukawa, H. (1982). *"Tabibito" (The Traveler)* (Singapore: World Scientific).

Zee, A. (1986). *Fearful Symmetry: The Search for Beauty in Modern Physics* (New York: Macmillan).

THE SCIENCES OF COMPLEXITY AND "ORIGINS OF ORDER"

STUART A. KAUFFMAN

INTRODUCTION

A new science, the science of complexity, is birthing. This science boldly promises to transform the biological and social sciences in the forthcoming century. My own book, *Origins of Order: Self Organization and Selection in Evolution*,[1] is at most one strand in this transformation. In this essay I shall characterize the book, but more important, set it in the broader context of the emerging sciences of complexity. Although the book is not yet out of the publisher's quiet womb, my own thinking has moved beyond that which I had formulated even a half year ago. Meanwhile, in the broader scientific community, the interest in "complexity" is exploding.

A summary of my own evolving intuition is this: In a deep sense, *Escherichia coli* and IBM know their respective worlds in the same way. Indeed, *E. coli* and IBM have each participated in the coevolution of entities which interact with and know one another. The laws which govern the emergence of knower and known, which govern the boundedly rational, optimally complex biological and social actors which have coformed, lie at the core of the science of complexity. This new body of thought implies that the poised coherence, precarious, subject to avalanches of change, of our biological and social world is inevitable. Such systems, poised on the edge of chaos, are the natural talismans of adaptive order.

The history of this emerging paradigm conveniently begins with the "cybernetic" revolution in molecular biology wrought by the stunning discoveries in 1961 and 1963 by later Nobelists François Jacob and Jacques Monod[2,3] that genes in the humble bacterium E. coli literally turn one another on and off. This discovery laid the foundation for the still-sought solution of the problem of cellular differentiation in embryology. The embryo begins as a fertilized egg, the single-cell zygote. Over the course of embryonic development in a human, this cell divides about fifty times, yielding the thousand trillion cells which form the newborn. The central mystery of developmental biology is that these trillions of cells become radically different from one another, some forming blood cells, others liver cells, still others nerve, gut, or gonadal cells. Previous work had shown that all the cells of a human body contain the same genetic instructions. How, then, could cells possibly differ so radically?

Jacob and Monod's discovery hinted at the answer. If genes can turn one another on and off, then cell types differ because different genes are expressed in each cell type. Red blood cells have hemoglobin, immune cells synthesize antibody molecules, and so forth. Each cell might be thought of as a kind of cybernetic system with complex genetic-molecular circuits orchestrating the activities of some 100,000 or more genes and their products. Different cell types, then, in some profound sense, calculate how they should behave.

THE EDGE OF CHAOS

My own role in the birth of the sciences of complexity begins in the same years, when as a medical student I asked an unusual, perhaps radical, question. Can the vast, magnificent order seen in development conceivably arise as a spontaneous self-organized property of complex genetic systems? Why "radical"? It is, after all, not the answers which scientists uncover, but the strange magic lying behind the questions they pose to their world, knower and known, which is the true impulse driving conceptual transformation. Answers will be found, contrived, wrested, once the question is divined. Since Darwin, we have viewed organisms, in Jacob's phrase, as bricolage, tinkered-together contraptions. Evolution, says Monod, is "chance caught on the wing." Lovely dicta, these, capturing the core of the Darwinian worldview in which organisms are perfected by natural selection acting on random variations. The tinkerer is an opportunist, its natural artifacts are *ad hoc* accumulations of this and that, molecular Rube Goldbergs satisfying some spectrum of design constraints.

In the worldview of bricolage, selection is the sole, or if not sole, the preeminent source of order. Further, if organisms are *ad hoc* solutions to design problems, there can be no deep theory of order in biology, only the careful dissection of the ultimately accidental machine and its ultimately accidental evolutionary history.

The genomic system linking the activity of thousands of genes stands at the summit of 4 billion years of an evolutionary process in which the specific genes, their regulatory inter-twining, and the molecular logic have all stumbled forward by random mutation and natural selection. Must selection have struggled against vast odds to create order? Or did that order lie to hand for selection's further molding? If the latter, then what a reordering of our view of life is mandated!

Order, in fact, lies to hand. Our intuitions have been wrong for thousands of years. We must, in fact, revise our view of life. Complex molecular regulatory networks inherently be-have in two broad regimes separated by a third phase-transition regime: The two broad regimes are chaotic and ordered. The phase-transition zone between these two comprises a narrow third complex regime poised on the boundary of chaos. Twenty-five years after the initial discovery of these regimes, a summary statement is that the genetic systems controlling ontogeny in mouse, human, bracken, fern, fly, bird—all—appear to lie in the ordered regime near the edge of chaos. Four billion years of evolution in the capacity to adapt offers a putative answer: complex adaptive systems achieve, in a lawlike way, the edge of chaos.

Tracing the history of this discovery, the discovery that extremely complex systems can exhibit "order for free," that our intuitions have been deeply wrong, begins with the intuition that even randomly "wired" molecular regulatory "circuits" with random "logic" would exhibit orderly behavior if each gene or molecular variable were controlled by only a few others. Notebooks from that period mix wire-dot diagrams of organic molecules serving as drugs with wire-dot models of genetic circuitry. The intuition proved correct. Idealizing a gene as "on" or "off," it was possible by computer simulations to show that large systems with thousands of idealized genes behaved in orderly ways if each gene is directly controlled by only two other genes. Such systems spontaneously lie in the ordered regime. Networks with many inputs per gene lie in the chaotic regime. Real genomic systems have few molecular inputs per gene, reflecting the specificity of molecular simplicity, to control the on/off behavior of those genes. Constraint to the vast ensemble of possible genomic systems characterized by these "local constraints" also inevitably yields genomic systems in the ordered regime. The perplexing, enigmatic, magical order of ontogeny may largely reflect large-scale consequences of polymer chemistry.

Order for free. But more: the spontaneously ordered features of such systems parallel a host of ordered features seen in the ontogeny of mouse, human, bracken, fern, fly, bird. A "cell type" becomes a stable recurrent pattern of gene expression, an "attractor" in the jargon of mathematics, where an attractor, like a whirlpool, is a region in the state space of all the possible patterns of gene activities to which the system flows and remains. In the spontaneously ordered regime, such cell-type attractors are inherently small, stable, and few, implying that the cell types of an organism traverse their recurrent patterns of gene expression in hours not eons, that homeostasis lies inevitably available for selection to mold, and, remarkably, that it should be possible to predict the number of cell types, each a whirlpool attractor in the genomic repertoire, in an organism. Bacteria harbor one to two cell types, yeast three, ferns and bracken some dozen, humans about two hundred and fifty. Thus, as the number of genes, called genomic complexity, increases, the number of cell types increases. Plotting cell types against genomic complexity, one finds that the number of cell types increases as a square-foot function of the number of genes. And the number of whirlpool attractors in model genomic systems in the ordered regime also increases as a square-root function of the number of genes. Humans, with about 100,000 genes, should have 317 cell types, close to 250. A simple alternative theory would predict billions of cell types.[1,4]

Bacteria, yeast, ferns, and humans, members of different phyla, have no common ancestor for the past 600 million years or more. Has selection struggled for 600 million years to achieve a square-root relation between genomic complexity and number of cell types? Or is this order for free so deeply bound into the roots of biological organization that selection cannot avoid this order? But if the latter, then selection is not the sole source of order in biology. Then Darwinism must be extended to embrace self-organization *and* selection.

The pattern of questions posed here is novel in biology since Darwin. In the Neo-Darwinian world view, where organisms are *ad hoc* solutions to design problems, the answers lie in the specific details wrought by ceaseless selection. In contrast, the explanatory approach offered by the new analysis rests on examining the statistically typical, or generic, properties of an entire class, or "ensemble," of systems all sharing known local features of genomic systems. If the typical, generic, features of ensemble members correspond to those seen in organisms, then an explanation of those features emphatically does not rest in the details. It rests in the general laws governing the typical features of the ensemble as a whole. Thus an "ensemble" theory is a new kind of statistical mechanics. It predicts that the typical properties of members of the ensemble will be found in organisms. Where true, it bodes a physics of biology.

Not only a physics of biology, but beyond, such a new statistical mechanics demands a new pattern of thinking with respect to biological and even cultural evolution: self-organization, yes, aplenty. But selection, or its analogues such as profitability, is always acting. We have no theory in physics, chemistry, biology, or beyond which marries self-organization and selection. The marriage consecrates a new view of life.

But two other failures of Darwin, genius that he was, must strike us. How do organisms, or other complex entities, manage to adapt and learn? That is, what are the conditions of "evolvability"? Second, how do complex systems coordinate behavior, and more deeply, why are adaptive systems so often complex?

Consider "evolvability" first. Darwin supposed that organisms evolve by the successive accumulation of useful random variations. Try it with a standard computer program. Mutate the code, scramble the order of instructions, and try to "evolve" a program calculating some complex function. If you do not chuckle, you should. Computer programs of the familiar type are not readily "evolvable." Indeed the more compact the code, the more lacking in redundancy, the more sensitive it is to each minor variation. Optimally condensed codes are, perversely, minimally evolvable. Yet the genome is a kind of molecular computer, and clearly has succeeded in evolving. But this implies something very deep: selection must achieve the kinds of systems which are able to adapt. That capacity is not God-given, it is a success.

If the capacity to evolve must itself evolve, then the new sciences of complexity seeking the laws governing complex adapting systems must discover the laws governing the emergence and character of systems which can themselves adapt by accumulation of successive useful variations.

But systems poised in the ordered regime near its boundary are precisely those which can, in fact, evolve by successive minor variations. The behavior of systems in the chaotic regime is so drastically altered by any minor variation in structure or logic that these systems cannot accumulate useful variations. Conversely, systems deep in the ordered regime are changed so slightly by minor variations that they adapt too slowly to an environment which may sometimes alter catastrophically.

Evolution of the capacity to adapt would be expected, then, to achieve systems poised near the edge of chaos.

How can complex systems coordinate behavior? Again, complex adaptive entities should achieve the edge of chaos because such systems can coordinate the most complex behavior there. Deep in the chaotic regime, alteration in the activity of any element in the system unleashes an avalanche of changes, or "damage," which propagates throughout most of the system. Such spreading damage is equivalent to the "butterfly effect" or sensitivity to initial conditions typical of chaotic systems. The butterfly in Rio changes the weather in Chicago. Crosscurrents of such avalanches unleashed from different elements mean that behavior is not controllable. Conversely, deep in the ordered regime, alteration at one point in the system alters only the behavior of a few neighboring elements. Signals cannot propagate widely throughout the system. Thus, control of complex behavior cannot be achieved. Just at the boundary between order and chaos, the most complex behavior can be achieved.

Finally, computer simulations suggest that natural selection or its analogues actually do achieve the edge of chaos. This third regime, poised between the broad ordered regime and the vast chaotic regime, is razor-blade thin in the space of systems. Absent other forces, randomly assembled systems will lie in the ordered or chaotic regime. But let such systems play games with one another, winning and losing as each system carries out some behavior with respect to the others, and let the structure and logic of each system evolve by mutation and selection, and, lo, systems do actually adapt toward the edge of chaos! No minor point this: evolution itself appears to bring complex systems, when they must adapt to the actions of others, to an internal structure and logic poised between order and chaos.

We are led to a bold hypothesis: complex adaptive systems achieve the edge of chaos.

The story of the "edge of chaos" is stronger, the implications more surprising. Organisms, economic entities, nations, do not evolve, they coevolve. Almost miraculously, coevolving systems, too, may mutually achieve the poised edge of chaos. Coevolution is the stuff of biological evolution. The sticky tongue of the frog alters the fitness of the fly, and deforms its fitness landscapes—that is, what directions of change in the fly's phenotype improve its chance of survival? But coevolution arises in technological evolution. The automobile replaced the horse. With the automobile came paved roads, gas stations (hence a petroleum industry and war in the Gulf), traffic lights, traffic courts, and motels. With the horse went stables, the smithy, and carriages. New goods and services alter the economic landscape. Coevolution is a story of coupled deforming "fitness landscapes." The outcome depends jointly on how much my landscape is deformed when you make an adaptive move, and how rapidly I can respond by changing "phenotype."

Are there laws governing coevolution? And how might they relate to the edge of chaos? In startling ways. Coevolution, due to a selective "metadynamics" tuning the structure of fitness landscapes and couplings between them, may typically reach the edge of chaos. *E. coli* and IBM not only "play" games with the other entities with which they coevolve, each also participates in the very definition or form of the game. It is we who create the world we mutually inhabit and in which we struggle to survive. In models where players can "tune" the mutual game even as they play, or coevolve, according to the game existing at any period, the entire system sometimes moves to the edge of chaos. This surprising result, if general, is of paramount importance.

Under this selective metadynamics, each entity tunes its own landscape structure and susceptibility to its own selfish advantage. As if by an invisible hand, model coevolving systems of such agents actually evolve toward the edge of chaos. Here, under most circumstances, most entities optimize fitness, or payoff, by remaining the same. Most of the ecosystem is frozen into a percolating Nash equilibrium, while coevolutionary changes propagate in local unfrozen islands within the ecosystem. More generally, alterations in circumstances send avalanches of changed optimal strategies propagating through the coevolving system. At the edge of chaos the size distributions of those avalanches approach a power law, with many small avalanches and few large ones. During such coevolutionary avalanches, affected players would be expected to fall transiently to low fitness, and hence might go extinct. Remarkably, this size distribution comes close to fitting the size distribution of extinction events in the evolutionary record. At a minimum, a distribution of avalanche sizes from a common-size small cause tells us that small and large extinction events may reflect endogenous features of coevolving systems rather than the size of the meteor which struck.

The implications are mini-Gaia. As if by an invisible hand, coevolving complex entities may mutually attain the poised boundary between order and chaos. Here, mean sustained payoff, or fitness is optimized. But here avalanches of change on all length scales can propagate through the poised system. The coevolution of complex adaptive entities itself may be lawful.

This strand in the birth of complexity theory, here spun, has its history. The first stages were set in the mid-1960s by the discovery of spontaneous order, as well as the expected chaos, in complex genomic systems. The discovery was not without attention among scientists of the day. Warren McCulloch, patriarch of cybernetics, author with Pitts of *The Logical Calculus of Ideas Imminent in the Mind,* stepchild of Bertrand Russell's logical atomism, and ancestor to today's neural connectionist tony flowering, invited me to share his home with his remarkable wife, Rook. "In pine tar is. In oak none is. In mud eels are. In clay none are," sang this poet of neural circuitry, demonstrating by dint of a minor Scots accent that no listener could unscramble four simple declarative sentences. Mind, complex, could fail to classify. "All Cambridge excited about your work," wrote McCulloch to this medical student who, thrilled, had yet to decode Warren's style.

Yet the time was not ripe. McCulloch had said twenty years would elapse before biologists took serious note. He was right, almost to the hour. And for good reason had he made his prediction. The late 1960s witnessed the blunderbuss wonderful explosion of molecular biology. Enough, far more than enough, to thrill to the discovery of the real molecular details: how a gene is transcribed to RNA, translated to protein, acts on its neighbors. What is the local logic of a bacterial genetic circuit controlling metabolism of lactose? Of a bacterial virus, or phage? What of the genes in a higher organism like the heralded but diminutive fruit fly? What of mouse and human? Enveloped by the Darwinian world view, whose truths run deep, held in tight thrall by the certainty that the order in organisms resides in the well-wrought details of construction and design, details inevitably *ad hoc* by virtue of their tinkered origins in the wasteland of chance, molecular biologists had no use for heady, arcane, abstract ensemble theories. The birth of complexity theory, or this strand of it, though noted, received no sustaining passion from its intended audience.

Twenty years, indeed. Rebirth of this strand was midwifed by the physicists. An analogue ensemble theory, called "spin glasses," had been developed starting in the mid-1970s by solid-state physicists such as Philip Anderson, Scott Kirkpatrick, Bernard Derrida, and Gerard Toulouse, struggling with an odd kind of dilute magnet material. Unlike the familiar ferromagnet, captured in the famous Ising model, where magnetic spins like to orient in the same direction as their neighboring spins, hence the attainment of the magnetized state with all spins oriented in the same direction, in these bewildering spin glasses adjacent spins might like to orient in the same or in the opposite direction, depending sinusoidally on the distance between the spins. What a mess. Edwards and Anderson started an industry among their brethren, and legitimized the new class of ensemble theories, by building mathematical models of spin glasses on two- or three-dimensional lattices.[5] Here each vertex houses a spin. But, to capture the bizarre logic of their magnetic materials, Edwards and Anderson assumed that each adjacent pair of spins "chose," once and forever, whether they wanted to point in the same or the opposite direction, and how much they cared, given by an energy for that bond. Such messy models meant two major things. First, since couplings are assigned at random, any one model spin glass is a member of a vast ensemble governed by the same statistics. This is an ensemble theory averaging not over the states of one system as in the familiar statistical mechanics of gases, but over billions of systems in the same ensemble. One seeks and characterizes the typical, or generic, features of these systems. Second, such systems have tortuous and rugged "energy landscapes." This is due to "frustration." Consider four spins around a square, where three adjacent pairs of spins wish to point in the same direction, the fourth pair does not. All cannot be satisfied. Each configuration of the many spins in the lattice of a spin glass has a total energy. The distribution of energies over the configurations is the energy landscape, the analogue of a fitness landscape. Frustration implies that the landscape is rugged and multipeaked.

Later, the structures of these spin glass landscapes would provide new models of molecular evolution over rugged multipeaked fitness landscapes.[1,6] Molecular evolution turns out to be much like an electron bouncing on a complex potential surface at a small temperature. At too low a temperature, the electron remains trapped in poor potential wells. At too high a temperature, the electron bounces all over the potential surface and has a high, unhappy, average energy. On any defined time scale, energy is minimized at a specific fixed temperature at which the electron is just "melting" out over the energy landscape, sliding gracefully over low saddles in the surface separating wells such that it finds good potential wells rather easily, then does not hop out of them too rapidly. The analogue in molecular evolution or other biological evolution over a fixed fitness landscape, or one deforming at a given mean rate, is to tune the parameters of adaptive search over the space such that an adapting population is just "melting" out of local regions of the space. Again: the edge of chaos!

By 1985 many of the physicists had tired of their spin glasses. Some turned to models of neural networks, sired by McCulloch, where neurons turn one another on and off rather like genes, or like spins for that matter. Hopfield found further fame by modeling parallel processing neural networks as spin systems.[7] Attractors of such networks, rather than modeling cell types as I had suggested, were taken to model memories.

Each memory was an attractor. Memories were content addressable, meaning that if the network were begun in the "basin of attraction" drained by one whirlpool attractor, the system would flow to that attractor. Partial data, corresponding to an initial state in a basin of attraction but not on the attractor itself, could be reconstructed to the stored memory. Toulouse, brilliant as Hopfield, followed with other spin-glass-like models whose basins of attraction were, he said, more like French than English gardens. Many have followed, to the field's flowering.

Not all the physicists who tired of spin glasses turned to neurobiology. In the way of these things, French physicist Gerard Weishbuch was romantically involved with French mathematician Françoise Fogleman-Soulie. Françoise chose, as her thesis topic, the still poorly understood order found in "Kauffman nets."[8] Many theorems followed. Gerard's interest extended from Françoise and spin glasses to this strange hint of order for free. A summer in Jerusalem at the Haddasah Hospital with Henri Atlan, doctor, theoretical biologist, author of *Crystal and Smoke* with its search for order and adaptability, led to more results. Put these bizarre genetic network on lattices, where any good problem resides. See the order. Scale parameters. Find phase transitions and the scaling laws of critical exponents. A new world to this biologist. And Gerard shared an office in Paris with Bernard Derrida, nephew of deconstructionist Jacques. Bernard looked at these "Kauffman nets," the name is due to Derrida, and leaped to an insight no biologist would ever dare. Let the network be randomly rewired at each moment, creating an "annealed" model. Theorem followed theorem. No genome dances so Mad Hatterly. But the mathematics can. Phase transition assured. Order for free in networks of low connectivity. Analysis of sizes of basins of attraction, and of overlaps between attractors.[9] I lost a bottle of wine to Derrida, shared over dinner, on the first theorem.

Even I chimed in with a few theorems here and there: a mean field approach to the sizes of attractors, the existence of a connected set of elements that are "frozen" and do not twinkle on and off, which spans or percolates across the system.

This frozen component, leaving behind isolated twinkling unfrozen islands, is the hallmark of order. The phase transition to chaos occurs, as parameters alter, when the frozen component "melts," and the twinkling islands merge into an unfrozen, twinkling, percolating sea, leaving behind small isolated frozen islands. The third, complex regime, the boundary between order and chaos, arises when the twinkling, connected, percolating, unfrozen sea is just breaking up into isolated islands. Avalanches of changes due to perturbations, which only propagate in the twinkling unfrozen sea, show a characteristic "power-law" distribution at the phase transition, with many small avalanches and a few enormous ones.[1,10]

Now the reader can see why systems on the boundary between order and chaos can carry out the most complex tasks, adapt in the most facile fashion. Now too, I hope, you can see the intrigue at the possibility that complex adaptive systems achieve the edge of chaos in their internal structure, but may also coevolve in a selective metadynamics to achieve the edge of chaos in the ecosystem of the mutual games they play! The edge of chaos may be a major organizing principle governing the evolution and coevolution of complex acaptive systems.

Other themes, again spawned by physicists, arose in America, and led quasi-independently, quasi-conversing, to the growth of interest in complexity. "Kauffman nets," where the wiring diagram among "genes," or binary elements, is random, and the logic governing each element, which is randomly assigned and hence differs for different "genes," are versions of a mathematical structure called "cellular automata." Cellular automata were invented by von Neuman, whose overwhelming early work, here and on the existence of self-reproducing automata, filters down through much that follows. The simplest cellular automata are lines or rings of on/off sites, each governed by the same logical rule which specifies its next activity, on or off, as a function of its own current state and those of its neighbors to a radius, r. Enter young Stephen Wolfram, quick, mercurial, entreprenurial. The youngest MacArthur Fellow, Wolfram had begun publishing in high-energy physics at age sixteen. While a graduate student at Cal

Tech, he earned the mixed admiration and enmity of his elders by inventing a computer code to carry out complex mathematical calculations. Cal Tech did not mind his mind. It minded his marketing the products of his mind. Never mind. Thesis done, Wolfram packed off to the Institute for Advanced Study and fell to the analysis of cellular automata (CA). He amazed his audiences. The world of oddball mathematicians, computer scientists, wayward physicists, and biologists soon twiddled with CA rules. Four classes of behavior emerged, stable, periodic, and chaotic, of course. And between them, on the edge between order and chaos, capable of complex computation—perhaps universal computation?—a fourth "complex class." Among the most famous of these CA rules is Conway's "Game of Life," provably capable of universal computation, demonstrably capable of capturing gigabits of memory and gigaseconds of time among amateurs and professionals worldwide. The game of life, like true life itself according to our bold hypothesis, also lies at the edge of chaos.

Paralleling Derrida is an independent lineage flowing from Chris Langton.[11] Langton, a computer scientist and physicist, elder graduate student, thought he could improve on von Neuman. He invented a simple self-reproducing automaton and littered computer screens from Los Alamos to wherever. Then Langton, following von Neuman again, and fired up by Wolfram, began playing with cellular automata. Where I had shown that the transition from order to chaos was tuned by tuning the number of inputs per "gene" from two to many, Langton independently and essentially simultaneously with Derrida, reinvented a classification of logical rules first promulgated by Crayton Walker. This classification marks the bias, P, toward the active, or inactive, state, over all combinations of activities of the inputs to an element. Derrida had shown that the phase transition occurred at a critical value of this bias, P_c. Langton found the same phase transition, but measured in a different way to focus on how complex a computation might be carried out in such a network. This complexity, measured as mutual information, or what one can predict about the next activity of one site given the activity of another site, is maximized at the phase transition. Langton, more than anyone, deserves credit for focusing attention on the computational capacities of systems at the edge of chaos.

The poised edge reappears, like a new second law of thermodynamics, everywhere hinted, but, without Carnot, not yet clearly articulated, in the recent work of physicist Jim Crutchfield. "Symbolic dynamics" is a clever new tool used to think about complex dynamical systems. Imagine a simple system such as a pendulum. As it swings back and forth, it crosses the midpoint where it hangs straight down. Use a 1 to denote times when the pendulum is to the left of the midpoint, and 0 to denote times when the pendulum swings to the right. Obviously, the periodic pendulum gives rise to an alternating sequence of 1 and 0 values. Such a symbol sequence records the dynamics of the pendulum by breaking its state space into a finite number of regions, here two, and labeling each region with a symbol. The flow of the system gives rise to a symbol sequence. Theorems demonstrate that, with optimally chosen boundaries between the regions, here the midpoint, the main features of the dynamics of the real pendulum can be reconstructed from the symbol sequence. For a periodic process, the symbol sequence is dull. But link several pendulums together with weak springs and again denote the behavior of one pendulum by 1 and 0 symbols. Now the motion of each pendulum is influenced by all the others in very complex ways. The symbol sequence is correspondingly complex. The next step is to realize that any symbol sequence can be generated as the output of a finite automaton, a more or less complex "neural" or "genetic" network of on/off elements. Further, theorems assure us that for any such symbol sequence, the smallest, or minimal, automaton, with the minimal number of elements and internal states, can be found. Thus, the number of elements, or states, of such a system is a measure of the complexity of the symbol sequence. And now the wonderful surprise. The same three phases, ordered, chaotic, and complex, are found again. That is, such automata, like cellular automata, Kauffman nets, and neural nets, harbor the same genetic behaviors. And, as you will now suspect, the complex regime again corresponds to the most complex symbol sequences, which in turn arise in dynamical systems themselves on the boundary between order and chaos.

If one had to formulate, still poorly articulated, a candidate general law of adaptation in complex systems, it might be this: life adapts to the edge of chaos.

THE ORIGIN OF LIFE AND ITS PROGENY

This story, the story of the boundary between order and chaos achieved by complex coevolving systems, is but half the emerging tale. The second voice tells of the origin of life itself, a story both testable and, I hope, true, a story implying vast stores of novel drugs, vaccines, universal enzymatic toolboxes, a story latent with the telling of technological and cultural evolution, of bounded rationality, the coemergence of knower and known, hence at last, of telling whether *E. coli* and IBM do, in fact, know their worlds, the worlds they themselves created, in the same deep way.

Life is held to be a miracle, God's breath on the still world, yet cannot be. Too much the miracle, then we were not here. There must be a viewpoint, a place to stand, from which the emergence of life is explicable, not as a rare untoward happening, but as expected, perhaps inevitable. In the common view, life originated as a self-reproducing polymer such as RNA or DNA, whose self-complementary structure, as Watson and Crick remarked with uncertain modesty, suggests its mode of reproduction. Yet stubbornly resistant to testing, to birthing *in vitro,* is this supposed simplest molecule of life. No worker has yet succeeded in getting one single-stranged RNA to line up the complementary free nucleotides, link them together to form the second strand, melt them apart, then repeat the cycle. The closest approach shows that a polyC polyG strand, richer in C than G, can in fact line up its complementary strand. Malevolently, the newly formed template is richer in G than C, and fails, utterly, to act as a facile template on its own. Alas.

Workers attached to the logic of molecular complementarity are now focusing their efforts on polymers other than RNA, polymers plausibly formed in the prebiotic environment, which might dance the still-sought dance. Others, properly entranced with the fact that RNA can act as an enzyme, called a ribozyme, cleaving and ligating RNA sequences apart and together, seek a ribozyme which can glide along a second RNA, serving as a template that has lined up its nucleotide complements, and zipper them together. Such a ribozyme would be a ribozyme polymerase, able to copy any RNA molecule, including itself. Beautiful indeed. And perhaps such a molecule occurred at curtain rise or early in the first act. But consider this: a free living organism, even the simplest bacterium, links the synthesis and degradation of some thousands of molecules in the complex molecular traffic of metabolism to the reproduction of the cell itself. Were one to begin with the RNA urbeast, a nude gene, how might it evolve? How might it gather about itself the clothing of metabolism?

There is an alternative approach which states that life arises as a nearly inevitable phase transition in sufficiently complex chemical systems—life, in this view, is formed by the emergence of a collectively autocatalytic system of polymers and simple chemical species.[1,12]

Picture, strangely, ten thousand buttons scattered on the floor. Begin to connect these at random with red threads. Every now and then, hoist a button and count how many buttons you can lift with it off the floor. Such a connected collection is called a "component" in a "random graph." A random graph is just a set of buttons connected at random by a set of threads. More formally, it is a set of N nodes connected at random by E edges. Random graphs undergo surprising phase transitions. Consider the ratio of E/N, or threads divided by buttons. When E/N is small, say 0.1, any button is connected directly or indirectly to only a few other buttons. But when E/N passes 0.5, so there are half as many threads as buttons, a phase transition has occurred. If a button is picked up, very many other buttons are picked up with it. In short, a "giant component" has formed in the random graph in which most buttons are directly or indirectly connected with one another. In short, connect enough nodes and a connected web "crystallizes."

Now life. Proteins and RNA molecules are linear polymers built by assembling a subset of monomers, twenty types in proteins, four in RNA. Consider the set of polymers up to some length, M, say 10. As M increases, the number of types of polymers increases exponentially; for example, there are 20^M proteins of length M. This is a familiar idea. The remaining ideas are less familiar. The simplest reaction among two polymers consists in gluing them together. Such reactions are reversible, so the converse reaction is simply cleaving a polymer into two shorter polymers. Now count the number of such reactions among the many polymers up to length M. A simple consequence of the combinatorial character of polymers is that there are many more reactions among the polymers than there are polymers. For example, a polymer of length M can be formed in $M - 1$ ways by gluing together shorter fragments comprising that polymer. Indeed, as M increases, the ratio of reactions among the polymers to polymers is about M, and hence increases as M increases. Picture such reactions as black, not red, threads running from the two smaller fragments to a small square "Reaction" box, then to the larger polymer made of them. Any such triad of black threads denotes a possible reaction among the polymers; the box, assigned a unique number, labels the reaction itself. The collection of all such triads is the chemical reaction graph among them. As the length of the longest polymer under consideration, M, increases, the web of black triads among these grows richer and richer. The system is rich with cross-linked reactions.

Life is an autocatalytic process where the system synthesizes itself from simple building blocks. Thus, in order to investigate the conditions under which such an autocatalytic system might spontaneously form, assume that no reaction actually occurs unless that reaction is catalyzed by some molecule. The next step notes that protein and RNA polymers can in fact catalyze reactions cleaving and ligating proteins and RNA polymers: trypsin in your gut after dinner digesting steak, or ribozyme ligating RNA sequences. Build a theory showing the probability that any given polymer can act as a catalyst for any given reaction. A simple hypothesis is that each polymer has a fixed chance, say one in a billion, to catalyze each reaction. No such theory can now be accurate, but this hardly matters. The conclusion is at hand, and insensitive to the details. Ask each polymer in the system, according to your theory, whether it catalyzes each possible reaction. If "yes," color the corresponding reaction triad "red," and note down which polymer catalyzed that reaction. Ask this question of all polymers for each reaction. Then some fraction of the black triads have become red. The red triads are the catalyzed reactions in the chemical reaction graph. But such a catalyzed reaction graph undergoes the button thread phase transition. When enough reactions are catalyzed, a vast web of polymers are linked by catalyzed reactions. Since the ratio of reactions to polymers increases with M, at some point as M increases at least one reaction per polymer is catalyzed by some polymer. The giant component crystallizes. An autocatalytic set which collectively catalyzes its own formation lies hovering in the now pregnant chemical soup. A self-reproducing chemical system, daughter of chance and number, swarms into existence, a connected, collectively autocatalytic metabolism. No nude gene, life emerged whole at the outset.

I found this theory in 1971. Even less than order for free in model genomic systems did this theory find favor. Stuart Rice, colleague, senior chemist, member of the National Academy of Sciences, asked, "What for?" Alas again. When famous older scientists say something warrants the effort, rejoice. When famous older scientists are dismissive, beware.

In 1983 interest in serious theories of the origin of life was rekindled. In 1971 and the ensuing decade, Nobelist Manfred Eigen, together with theoretical chemist Peter Schuster, developed a well-formulated, careful model of the origin of life, called the "hypercycle."[13] In this theory, the authors begin by assuming that short nude RNA sequences can replicate themselves. The hook is this: during such replication, errors are made. The wrong nucleotide may be incorporated at any site.

Eigen and Schuster showed that an error catastrophe occurs when RNA sequences become too long for any fixed error rate. The RNA population "melts" over RNA sequence space; hence all information accumulated within the "best" RNA sequence, culled by natural selection, is lost. The "hypercycle" is a clever answer to this devastation: assume a set of different short RNA molecules, each able to replicate itself. Now assume that these different RNA molecules are arranged in a control cycle, such that RNA 1 helps RNA 2 to replicate, RNA 2 helps RNA 3, and so on until RNA N closes the loop by helping RNA 1. Such a loop is a hypercycle, "hyper" because each RNA itself is a tiny cycle of two complementary strands which copy each other. The hypercycle is, in fact, a coevolving molecular society. Each RNA species coevolves in company with its peers. This model has been studied in detail, and has strengths and weaknesses. Not the least of the latter is that no experimental evidence demonstrated as yet that an RNA sequence can replicate itself.

But other voices were lifted, from the most intelligent minds. Freeman Dyson, of the Institute of Advanced Studies, an elegant scientist and author of lyric books such as *Disturbing the Universe,* suggested, in *Origins of Life,* that life arose as a phase transition in complex systems of proteins. Philip Anderson, with Daniel Stein and Rothkar, borrowed from spin glass theory to suggest that a collection of template-replicating RNA molecules with overlapping ends and complex fitness functions governing their survival might give rise to many possible self-reproducing sequences.

Lives in science have their peculiar romance. I heard of these approaches at a conference in India. Central India, Madya Pradesh, sweats with the sweet smell of the poor cooking over fires of dried buffalo dung. The spiritual character of India allows one to speak of the origin of life with colleagues such as Humberto Maturana, riding in disrepair except for his glasses and clear thoughts, in a bus of even greater disrepair among the buffalo herds to Sanchi, an early Buddhist shrine. The Buddha at the west portal, thirteen hundred years old, ineffably young, invited only a gentle kiss from the foreigners in time, space, culture. Dyson's and Anderson's approaches appeared flawed. Dyson appeared to have assumed his conclusion, hidden in assumption 7. Life as an autocatalytic crystallization was built into his model, slipped in by hand, not actually accounted for as an emergent property of chemistry. And Anderson, Stein, and Rothkar, while wonderfully insightful, based their model on RNA self-complementarity. I decided to try to formulate the original autocatalytic set model more precisely, and managed a few theorems, simple to any real mathematician.

This hiccup of creativity, I hoped, warranted investigation. Doyne Farmer, a young physicist at Los Alamos, and his childhood friend Norman Packard and I began collaborating to build detailed computer simulations of such autocatalytic polymer systems. Six years later, a fine Ph.D. thesis by Richard Bagley later, it is clear that the initial intuitions were fundamentally correct: in principle, complex systems of polymers can become collectively self-reproducing. The routes of life may not be twisted back alleys of thermodynamic improbability, but broad boulevards of combinatorial inevitability.

If this new view of the crystallization of life as a phase transition is correct, then it should soon be possible to create actual self-reproducing polymer systems, presumably of RNA or proteins, in the laboratory. Experiments, even now, utilizing very complex libraries of stochastic RNA molecules or polypeptides to search for autocatalytic sets, are feasible.

If not since Darwin, then since Weisman's doctrine of the germ plasm was reduced to molecular detail by the discovery of the genetic role of chromosomes, biologists have believed that evolution via mutation and selection virtually requires a stable genetic material as the store of heritable information. But mathematical analysis of model autocatalytic polymer systems belies this conviction. Such systems can evolve to form new systems. Thus, contrary to Richard Dawkin's thesis in *The Selfish Gene,* biological evolution does not, in principle, demand self-replicating genes at the base. Life can emerge and evolve without a genome. Heresy, perhaps? Perhaps.

Many and unexpected are the children of invention. Autocatalytic polymer sets have begotten an entire new approach to complexity. The starting point is obvious. An autocatalytic polymer set is a functional integrated whole. Given such a set, it is clear that one can naturally define the function of any given polymer in the set with respect to the capacity of the set to reproduce itself. Lethal mutants exist, for if a given polymer is removed, or a given foodstuff deleted, the set may fail to reproduce itself. Ecological interactions among coevolving autocatalytic sets lie to hand. A polymer from one such set injected into a second such set may block a specific reaction step and "kill" the second autocatalytic set. Coevolution of such sets, perhaps bounded by membranes, must inevitably reveal how such systems "know" one another, build internal models of one another, and cope with one another. Models of the evolution of knower and known lay over the conceptual horizon.

Walter Fontana, graduate student of Peter Schuster, came to the Santa Fe Institute, and Los Alamos. Fontana had worked with John McCaskill, himself an able young physicist collaborating with Eigen at the Max Planck Institute in Göttingen. McCaskill dreamt of polymers, not as chemicals, but as Turing machine computer programs and tapes. One polymer, the computer, would act on another polymer, the tape, and "compute" the result, yielding a new polymer. Fontana was entranced. But he also found the autocatalytic story appealing. Necessarily, he invented "algorithmic chemistry." Necessarily, he named his creation "alchemy."[14]

Alchemy is based on a language for universal computation called the lambda calculus. Here almost any binary symbol string is a legitimate "program" which can act on almost any binary symbol string as an input to compute an output binary symbol string. Fontana created a "Turing gas" in which an initial stock of symbol strings randomly encounter one another in a "chemostat" and may or may not interact to yield symbol strings. To maintain the analogue of selection, Fontana requires that a fixed total number of symbol string polymers be maintained in the chemostat. At each moment, if the number of symbol strings grows above the maximum allowed, some random strings are lost from the system.

Autocatalytic sets emerge again! Fontana finds two types. In one, a symbol string which copies itself emerges. This "polymerase" takes over the whole system. In the second, collectively autocatalytic sets emerge in which each symbol string is made by some other string or strings, but none copies itself. Such systems can then evolve in symbol string space—evolution without a genome.

Fontana had broken the bottleneck. Another formulation of these ideas, which I am now using, sees interactions among symbol strings creating symbol strings and carrying out a "grammar." Work on disordered networks, work which exhibited the three broad phases, ordered, chaotic, and complex, drove forward based on the intuition that order and comprehensibility would emerge by finding the generic behavior in broad regions of the space of possible systems. The current hope is that analysis of broad reaches of grammar space, by sampling "random grammars," will yield important insight into this astonishingly rich class of systems.

The promise of these random grammar systems may extend from analysis of evolving proto-living systems to characterizing mental processes such as multiple personalities, the study of technological coevolution, and cultural evolution. And the origin of life model itself, based on the probability that an arbitrary protein catalyzes an arbitrary reaction, spawned the idea of applied molecular evolution—the radical concept that we might generate trillions of random genes, RNA sequences, and proteins, and learn to evolve useful polymers able to serve as drugs, vaccines, enzymes, and biosensors. The practical implications now appear large.[1]

Strings of symbols which act upon one other to generate strings of symbols can, in general, be computationally universal. That is, such systems can carry out any specified algorithmic computation. The immense powers and yet surprising limits, trumpeted since Gödel, Turing, Church, and Kleene, lie before us, but in a new and suggestive form. Strings acting on strings to generate strings create a novel conceptual framework in which to cast the world. The puzzle of mathematics, of course, is that it should so often be so outrageously useful in categorizing the world. New conceptual schemes allow starkly new questions to be posed.

A grammar model is simply specified. It suffices to consider a set of M pairs of symbol strings, each about N symbols in length. The meaning of the grammar, a catch-as-catch-can set of "laws of chemistry," is this: wherever the left member of such a pair is found in some symbol string in an independent "soup" of strings, substitute the right member of the pair. Thus, given an initial soup of strings, one application of the grammar might be carried out by us, acting godlike. We regard each string in the soup in turn, try all grammar rules in some precedence order, and carry out the transformations mandated by the grammar. Strings become strings become strings. But we can also let the strings themselves act on one another. Conceive of a string as an "enzyme" which acts on a second string as a "substrate" to produce a "product." A simple specification shows the idea. If a symbol sequence on a string in the soup, say 111, is identical to a symbol sequence on the "input" side of one grammar pair, then that 111 site in the string in the soup can act as an enzymatic site. If the enzymatic site finds a substrate string bearing the same site, 111, then the enzyme acts on the substrate and transforms its 111 to the symbol sequence mandated by the grammar, say 0101. Here, which symbol string in the soup acts as enzyme and which is substrate is decided at random at each encounter. With minor effort, the grammar rules can be extended to allow one enzyme string to glue two substrate strings together, or to cleave one substrate string into two product strings.

Grammar string models exhibit entirely novel classes of behavior, and all the phase transitions shown in the origin of life model. Fix a grammar. Start the soup with an initial set of strings. As these act on one another, it might be the case that all product strings are longer than all substrate strings. In this case, the system never generates a string previously generated.

Call such a system a jet. Jets might be finite, the generation of strings petering out after a while, or infinite. The set of strings generated from a sustained founder set might loop back to form strings formed earlier in the process, by new pathways. Such "mushrooms" are just the autocatalytic sets proposed for the origin of life. Mushrooms might be finite or infinite, and might, if finite, squirt infinite jets into string space. A set of strings might generate only itself, floating free like an egg in string space. Such an egg is a collective identity operator in the complex parallel processing algebra of string transformations. The set of transformations collectively specifies only itself. The egg, however, might wander in string space, or squirt an infinite jet. Perturbations to an egg, by injecting a new string, might be repulsed, leaving the egg unchanged, or might unleash a transformation to another egg, a mushroom, a jet. Similarly, injection of an exogenous string into a finite mushroom might trigger a transformation to a different finite mushroom, or even an infinite mushroom. A founder set of strings might galvanize the formation of an infinite set of strings spread all over string space, yet leave local "holes" in string space because some strings might not be able to be formed from the founder set. Call such a set a filigreed fog. It may be formally undecidable whether a given string can be produced from a founder set. Finally, all possible strings might ultimately be formed, creating a pea soup in string space.

Wondrous dreamlike stuff, this. But more lies to hand. Jets, eggs, filigreed fogs, and the like are merely the specification of the string contents of such an evolving system, not its dynamics. Thus, an egg might regenerate itself in a steady state, in a periodic oscillation during which the formation of each string waxes and wanes cyclically, or chaotically. The entire "edge of chaos" story concerned dynamics only, not composition. String theory opens new conceptual territory.

NEW TERRITORY

Models of mind, models of evolution, models of technological transformation, of cultural succession, these grammar models open new provinces for precise thought. I turn next in this essay to mention their possible relation to artificial intelligence and connectionism, sketch their possible use in the philosophy of science, then discuss their use in economics, where they may provide an account of technological evolution.

Not the least of these new territories might be a new model of mind. Two great views divide current theories of mind. In one, championed by traditional artificial intelligence, the mind carries out algorithms in which condition rules act on action rules to trigger appropriate sequences of actions. In contrast, connectionism posits neural networks whose attractors are classes, categories, or memories. The former are good at sequential logic and action, the latter are good at pattern recognition. Neither class has the strengths of the other. But parallel-processing symbol strings have the strength of both. More broadly, parallel-processing string systems in an open coevolving set of strings, wherein individuation of coordinated clusters of these production processes arises, may be near-universal models of minds, knower and known, mutually creating the world they inhabit.

Next, some comments about the philosophy of science by an ardent amateur. Since Quine we have lived with holism in science, the realization that some claims are so central to our conceptual web that we hold them well-nigh unfalsifiable, hence treat them as well-nigh true by definition. Since Kuhn we have lived with paradigm revolutions and the problems of radical translation, comparability of terms before and after the revolution, reducibility. Since Popper we have lived ever more uneasily with falsifiability and the injunction that there is no logic of questions. And for decades now we have lived with the thesis that conceptual evolution is like biological evolution: better variants are cast up, never mind how conceived, and passed through the filter of scientific selection. But we have no theory of centrality versus peripherality in our web of concepts, hence no theory of pregnant versus trivial questions, or of conceptual recastings which afford revolutions or wrinkles. But if we can begin to achieve a body of theory which accounts for both knower and known as entities which have coevolved with one another, *E. coli* and its world, IBM and its world, and understand what it is for such a system to have a "model" of its world via meaningful materials, toxins, foods, shadow of a hawk cast on newborn chick, we must be well on our way to understanding science too as a web creating and grasping a world.

Holism should be interpretable in statistical detail. The centrality of Newton's laws of motion compared to details of geomorphology in science find their counterpart in the centrality of the automobile and peripherality of Pet Rocks in economic life. Conceptual revolutions are like avalanches of change in ecosystems, economic systems, and political systems. We need a theory of the structure of conceptual webs and their transformation. Pregnant questions are those which promise potential changes propagating far into the web. We know a profound question when we see one. We need a theory, or framework, to say what we know. Like Necker cubes, alternative conceptual webs are alternative grasped worlds. We need a way to categorize "alternative worlds" as if they were alternative stable collective string production systems, eggs or jets. Are mutually exclusive conceptual alternatives, like multiple personalities, literally alternative ways of being in the world? What pathways of conceptual change flow from a given conceptual web to what "neighboring" webs, and why? This is buried in the actual structure of the web at any point. Again, we know this, but need a framework to say what we know. I suspect grammar models and string theory may help. And conceptual evolution is like cultural evolution. I cannot help the image of an isolated society with a self-consistent set of roles and beliefs as an egg shattered by contact with our supracritical Western civilization.

Now to economic webs, where string theory may provide tools to approach technological evolution. I should stress that this work is just beginning. The suspected conclusions reach beyond that which has been demonstrated mathematically or by simulations.

String theory may provide tools to approach the fundamental problem of technological evolution. Theoretical economists can earn a living scratching equations on blackboards. This is a strange way to catch dinner. One hundred thousand years ago, their ancestors scratched a living in a more direct way. Economists survive only because the variety of goods and services in an economy has expanded since Neanderthal times to include the services of mathematical economists. Why? And what role does the structure of an economic web play in its own growth?

The central idea is that, in fact, the structure of an economic web at any moment plays the central role in its own transformation to a new web with new goods and services and lacking old goods and services. But it is precisely this central fact that the economists have, until now, no coherent means to think about. The richness of economic webs has increased. The introduction of the automobile, as noted, unleased an avalanche of new goods and services ranging from gas stations to motels, and drove out horse, buggy, and the like. Economists treat technological evolution as "network externalities." This cumbersome phrase means that innovation is imagined to occur due to causes "outside" the economy. While innovation has cascading consequences of the utmost importance, traditional economic theory is not to account for technological evolution, but to note its history and treat such innovation as exogenous. Strange, since the bulk of economic growth in the current century is driven by innovation.

There is a profound reason why economics has had a difficult time building a theory of the evolution of technological webs. Economists lack a theory of technological complementarity and substitutability, without which no such web theory can be built. String theory may offer such a framework. Economists call nut and bolt, ham and eggs, "complements." That is, complements are goods and services which are used together for some purpose. Screw and nail are "substitutes"; each can replace the other for most purposes. But the growth of technological niches rests on which goods and services are complements and substitutes for one another. Thus, the introduction of the computer led to software companies because software and hardware are complements. Without a theory of which goods and services are complements and substitutes for one another, one cannot build a decent account of the way technological webs grow autocatalytically.

String theory may help. Any random grammar, drawn from the second-order infinite set of possible grammars, can be taken as a catch-as-catch-can model not only of the "laws of chemistry," but of the unknown "laws of technological complementarity and substitutability." Strings which act on strings to make strings are tools, or capital goods. The set of strings needed as inputs to a tool to make product strings is itself a set of complements. Each string is needed with the rest to make the products. Strings which can substitute for one another as inputs to a tool to yield the same products are substitutes for one another. Such complements and substitutes constitute the "production functions" of the economist, or, for consumption goods, the consumption complementarities and substitutions, ham and eggs, salt and potassium chloride.

We have no idea what the laws of technological complementarity and substitutability are, but by scanning across grammar space we are scanning across possible models of such laws. If vast regimes of grammar space yield similar model economic results, and we can map the regimes on to real economic systems, then those regimes of grammar space would capture, in an "as-if" fashion, the unknown laws of technological complementarity and substitutability which govern economic links. An ensemble theory again. Catch-as-catch-can can catch the truth.

These economic string models are now in use to study the evolution of technological webs. The trick is to calculate, at each period, which of the goods currently produced, or now rendered possible by innovation based on the current goods, are produced in the next period and which current goods are no longer produced. This allows studies of avalanches of technological change.

In more detail, an economic model requires production functions, an assignment of utility to each good or service, and budget constraints. An economic equilibrium is said to exist if a ratio of the amounts of goods and services produced is found which simultaneously optimizes utility and such that all markets clear—no bananas are left rotting on the dock, no hungry folk are hankering for unproduced pizzas. At each period those goods, old and newly possible, which are profitable are incorporated into the economy, and those old and new goods which would operate at a loss are not. Thus, these models are literally the first which will show the ways avalanches of goods and services come into and leave economic systems. Heretofore, the economists have lacked a way to say why, when an innovation (the automobile) enters, such and such numbers of other new goods are called into existence, while old goods are rendered obsolete. Now we can hope to study such transformations. The evolution of economic webs stands on the verge of becoming an integral feature of economic theory. Since such evolution dominates the economic growth of the late twentieth century and will dominate the economic growth of the early twenty-first century, the capacity to study such evolution is not merely of academic interest.

String theory provides possible new insights into economic takeoff. The twenty-first century will undoubtedly witness the encroaching struggle between North and South, developed and developing economies, to learn how to share wealth and, more essentially, learn how to trigger adequate economic growth in the South. For decades economists have sought adequate theories of economic takeoff. Typically these rest on the idea of accumulation of sufficient surplus to invest. But string theory suggests this picture may be inadequate. Summon all the surpluses one wishes, if the economic web is too simple in variety to allow the existing niches to call forth innovation to create novel goods and services, the economy will remain stagnant and not take off. In short, string theory suggests that an adequate complexity of goods and services is required for phase transition to take off.

These phase transitions are simply understood, and can depend upon the complexity of one model economy, or the onset of trade between two insufficiently complex economies. Think of two boxes, labeled France and England. Each has a forest of types of founder strings growing within it. If, in either country, the goods and services denoted by the founder strings are too simple, then the economy will form a faltering finite jet, which soon sputters out. Few novel goods are produced at first, then none. But if the complexity of goods and services within one country is great enough, then, like an autocatalytic set at the origin of life, it will explode into an indefinitely growing proliferation of goods and services, a mushroom, filigreed fog, etc. Thus, takeoff requires sufficient technological complexity that it can feed on itself and explode. It will occur in one economy if it is sufficiently complex. Or onset of trade can trigger takeoff. Let France and England be subcritical, but begin to exchange goods. The exchange increases the total complexity, and thus the growth of new opportunities and new niches for innovation, which may catapult the coupled economies to supracritical explosion. Takeoff.

CLOSING REMARK: A PLACE FOR LAWS IN HISTORICAL SCIENCES

I close this essay by commenting on Burian and Richardson's thoughtful review of *Origins of Order*. They properly stress a major problem: What is specifically "biological" in the heralded renderings of ensemble theories? This is a profound issue. Let me approach it by analogy with the hoped-for use of random grammar models in economics as discussed above. As emphasized, economists lack a theory of technological evolution because they lack a theory of technological complementarities and substitutes. One needs to know why nuts go with bolts to account for the coevolution of these two bits of econostuff. But we have no such theory, nor is it even clear what a theory which gives the actual couplings among ham and eggs, nuts and bolts, screws and nails, computer and software engineer, might be. The hope for grammar models is that each grammar model, one of a nondenumerably infinite set of such grammars since grammars map power sets of strings into power sets of strings, is a "catch-as-catch-can" model of the unknown laws of technological complementarity and substitutability. The hope is that vast reaches of "grammar space" will yield economic models with much the same global behavior. If such generic behaviors map on to the real economic world, I would argue that we have found the proper structure of complementarity and substitutability relationships among goods and services, and hence can account for many statistical aspects of economic growth. But this will afford no account of the coupling between specific economic goods such as power transmission and the advent of specific new suppliers to Detroit. Is such a theory specifically "economics"? I do not know, but I think so.

Grammar models afford us the opportunity to capture statistical features of deeply historically contingent phenomena ranging from biology to economics, perhaps to cultural evolution. Phase transitions in complex systems may be lawful, power law distributions of avalanches may be lawful, but the specific avalanches of change may not be predictable. Too many throws of the quantum dice. Thus we confront a new conceptual tool which may provide a new way of looking for laws in historical sciences. Where will the specifics lie? As always, I presume, in the consequences deduced after the axioms are interpreted.

NOTES

1. S. A. Kauffman, *Origins of Order: Self Organization and Selection in Evolution* (Oxford University Press, 1993).
2. F. Jacob & J. Monod, "On the Regulation of Gene Activity," *Cold Spring Harbor Symposia of Quantitative Biology*, 26 (1961): 193–211.
3. F. Jacob & J. Monod, "Genetic Repression, Allosteric Inhibition, and Cellular Differentiation," in *Cytodifferentiation and Macromolecular Synthesis,* edited by M. Locke, 21st Symposium of the

Society for the Study of Development and Growth (New York: Academic Press, 1963), pp. 30–64.

4. S. A. Kauffman, "Metabolic Stability and Epigenesis in Randomly Connected Nets," *Journal of Theoretical Biology,* 22 (1969): 437–467.

5. S. F. Edwards & P. W. Anderson, "Theory of Spin Glasses," *Journal of Physics,* 5 (1975): 965.

6. S. A. Kauffman, "Adaptation on Rugged Fitness Landscapes," in *Lectures in the Sciences of Complexity,* The Santa Fe Institute Series, edited by Dan Stein (Boston: Addison-Wesley, 1989).

7. J. J. Hopfield, "Neural Networks and Physical Systems with Emergent Collective Computational Abilities," *Proceedings of the National Academy of Sciences USA* 79 (1982): 2554–2558.

8. F. Fogleman-Soulie, "Parallel and Sequential Computation on Poolean Networks," in *Theoretical Computer Science,* Vol. 40 (New York: Elsevier/North Holland, 1985).

9. B. Derrida & Y. Pomeau, "Random Networks of Automata in Simple Annealed Approximation," *Europhysical Letters* 1, 2 (1986): 45–49.

10. S. A. Kauffman, "Principles of Adaptation in Complex Systems," in *Lectures in the Sciences of Complexity,* The Santa Fe Institute Series, edited by Dan Stein (Boston: Addison-Wesley, 1989).

11. C. Langton, "Life at the Edge of Chaos," in *Artificial Life II,* edited by Langton, Farmer, Taylor (Boston: Addison-Wesley, 1992) pp. 41–91.

12. S. A. Kauffman, "Autocatalytic Sets of Proteins," *Journal of Theoretical Biology,* 119 (1986): 1–24.

13. M. Eigen & P. Schuster, *The Hypercycle: A Principle of Natural Self Organization* (New York: Springer-Verlag, 1979).

14. W. Fontana, "Algorithmic Chemistry," in *Artificial Life II,* edited by Langton, Farmer, Taylor (Boston: Addision-Wesley, 1992) pp. 159–209.

GIVING IT AWAY AT THE MACARTHUR FELLOWS PROGRAM

KENNETH HOPE

"La façon de donner vaut mieux que ce qu'on donne."
—Pierre Corneille, *Le Menteur*

UPON LEAVING the MacArthur Fellows Program in 1992, I felt as if I had stepped ashore after spending many years on a sea voyage aboard some marvelous ship, sailing across vast oceans from one exotic port to another, meeting all kinds of wonderful people who do fantastic things. In many ways it was like having been on a treasure hunt—the difference being that the Program started with the pot of gold in hand. We set out almost fifteen years ago to discover and support some of America's most talented and promising ididuals. We looked everywhere—among poets and mathematicians, university professors and classroom teachers, Middle East scholars and field biologists, physicists and archaeologists, community organizers and anthropologists, environmentalists and filmmakers—searching for the persons who we felt best exemplified the values of the Program we had invented.[1]

The first announcement of 21 MacArthur Fellows was made in May of 1981; since then 383 individuals have been awarded five years of unrestricted support to do with as they wish.[2] With every announcement the press has had a field day, adding

108

dimensions to the Program we ourselves had not anticipated, and giving it a public identity. Although the Program is well known publicly, its roots are intensely personal, owing much of its character to one of its founders, J. Roderick MacArthur. It also derives much from the particular time in which it was developed. The Fellows Program has deliberately sought from the beginning to represent a diverse and pluralistic model of the concept of creativity. It represents an effort to celebrate creative individuals and to support them through long-term investment. For many people the Program has helped to define creativity through its selections, but it also exemplifies aspects of creativity in other ways. One of the characteristics of the kind of person we seek is a striving to define oneself for oneself through creative work. Perhaps now, as an observer, it is time for me to reflect on some of my experiences.

1.

In 1978 I began working with J. Roderick MacArthur on the invention of a new effort in philanthropy designed to enhance the social good by recognizing and supporting promising and creative individuals.[3] Our plan for the MacArthur Fellows Program evolved out of an interwoven set of beliefs:

- That society is enhanced and the quality of life is improved by the discoveries and creations of individuals working in all areas of human endeavor, including across disciplines.
- That individuals, rather than institutions, represent the critical node in discovery, invention, and creation.
- That individuals working to advance knowledge or solve problems are more effective and productive if given the opportunity to create and maintain their own working conditions over an extended period of time in relative freedom.
- That procedures for the selection of individuals are most effective when formulated by a group of committed experts from a variety of disciplines and backgrounds.

- That it is as important to support the process of work as it is to support the creation of specific products or outcomes.
- That the nature of the support is more important than the field or fields of endeavor in which the support is made.
- That a society that wishes to enhance its own human and productive capacities ought to establish significant prizes and public recognition of promising individuals.

The Fellows Program avoided defining the term "creativity" in any official capacity.[4] It would have been a mistake to do so, since defining what we meant by creativity within the context of the Program would have inhibited the scope of our inquiry. One of the Program's most successful characteristics has been its ability to call on thousands of experts in all areas. These people have applied their own definitions of creativity by recommending persons for the MacArthur Fellowship, or by commenting on those recommendations for the peer-review process. A single definition of creativity would have placed significant constraints on the ability of the Program to operate effectively both within and across fields. The Fellows Program is more about creative individuals than about creativity as a concept. As problematic as it is to define creativity, it is far more difficult to define the mental processes from which it derives.

We have worked with practitioners in the arts, the sciences, the social sciences, the humanities, and public affairs, building a flexible framework within which hundreds of different creative individuals of many ages, doing a range of work, can be evaluated, each on his or her own merits. The success of the Program depended on learning how to solicit and to accept or reject advice from people who knew more than we did about a particular topic or person.

The decision to look for individuals across fields was extremely important. At the time, many advisers urged us to limit our efforts to one field or another. By concentrating all our efforts in one specific area, we were told, we would give the Program a secure definition; a relatively well-defined body of research or activities in which to engage our support; a distinct group of institutions and individuals from within academia, nonprofits, and government to serve as advisers and recipients; and a framework within which our achievements as a grant-maker could be objectively and fairly evaluated by the target community and by society at large.

Instead, we invented a program that would search across the entire country for creative individuals, regardless of field. By doing so, we placed individuals above their disciplines. This shocked and annoyed many people at the time, and still does. The criteria we adopted include three elements: the work's importance to society, the individual's creativity and promise, and the award's enabling effect to the recipient. One of the most important early decisions was to set a high ceiling on the number of Fellows (not to exceed 200 over a five-year period). In practice, this gave the Program a broad enough scope to search widely without constraint.

We also decided that we would accept nominations only from designated nominators, who would request consideration for others they admired rather than for themselves. The idea to use nominators came—at least in part—from the work of Robert K. Merton, who called them the human counterparts to truffle dogs, after the animals trained to sniff out that delicacy.[5] We invited people to be nominators on the basis of their expertise, their devotion to excellence, and their recognition of quality work and potential in others. Additionally, we regarded many of the nominators as connoisseurs of talent and creativity.

2.

Let us consider the creation of the MacArthur Fellows Program. It begins, naturally, with the wealth of John D. MacArthur. Plato wrote that people who make fortunes love their money not simply for its use and profit, but with a second kind of love, which resembles that of poets for their own poems, or parents for their children, as "a creation of their own."[6] The task of the Board of Directors of the MacArthur Foundation was to sustain that sense by developing programs creatively and by identifying recipients on the basis of their creativity.

In the late 1970s, our society was in the midst of profound changes. It seemed that the traditional disciplines and methodologies which defined our culture were being wrenched apart, and that something new was being born. The emergent society took its shape from new considerations of race, gender, and social justice. More variable constructions of reality and knowledge led to a considerably more open and diverse approach to issues concerning the quality of human productions. Single or unitary conceptions of quality were replaced by more open and diverse attitudes.

The person most responsible for the idea behind the MacArthur Fellows Program was J. Roderick MacArthur, the son of the founder. Where did he get the idea for the Fellows Program? I would make the case that particular facets of Rod's life and character played a significant role in the creation of the Program. The official version of events records that the idea came from an article by Dr. George Burch, entitled "Of Venture Research," brought to the MacArthur Foundation's first Board of Directors meeting by William Kirby, who was John D. MacArthur's lawyer. As Bill Kirby would tell it later, Rod saw a good thing in Bill's suggestion and turned it to the Foundation's advantage. Bill outlived Rod by a number of years, and so had the advantage of time to retell his version of events, which was correct as far as it went. As Program Director, I confess to tailoring my own version of events to conform more with Kirby's than I might otherwise have done, because of his powerful presence on the Board of Directors. Since I was present at the beginning, what I remember is far more complex than Rod's picking up a good idea from Dr. Burch, let alone Bill Kirby, and running with it.

Rod had maintained a close but difficult relationship with his father throughout his life; as a result, he and Bill Kirby also clashed. When they both found themselves on the Board of this newly wealthy foundation, with no directions from the donor as to how to shape its philanthropy, each kept a wary eye on the other and regarded one another with deep suspicion and mistrust. For both of them John MacArthur had been a highly significant person they had been very close to; each acted as if he had a "pipeline to the grave." Some of this antagonism was due not simply to their instinctual mistrust, but to the mutual respect they had for each other's minds and capabilities. They were both extremely effective in manipulating events and people, both very powerful men used to having their way, and both highly intelligent.

The article by Dr. Burch which served as the efficient cause of the Fellows Program argued that

> there is a need for granting agencies to seek out investigators who are genuinely interested in research and exploration of the unknown to advance knowledge for the sake of knowledge. Recipients should be left alone without the annoyances and distractions imposed by grant applications, reviewing committees, and pressure to publish.[7]

Rod and I were aware that this kind of argument was being made regularly, particularly in the scientific and business communities.[8] There was a sense that things were going wrong at the "cutting edge" (a term Rod learned to despise). Individual creativity, it was said, was being stymied by too much concern for bureaucratic matters in grant applications. Individuals were being ignored in favor of institutions, and money went for already clearly defined projects rather than to individuals who came up with the ideas in the first place.[9] Most of this argument had a patriotic flavor—we would become a better country, more competitive and stronger, if we could devote our resources to creativity and creative individuals.

When Rod was made a board member of his father's foundation, he began to express a fervent belief that foundations had an obligation to do the things which only they could do. Rod championed foundations for their independent approach to the world's problems. Specifically, he thought that foundations should be doing the things government cannot and will not do. He assumed that government had certain obligations, and that even if these were not being met, it was not the business of foundations to "bail out" the government.

Rod MacArthur admired creativity, and felt instinctively that he himself was a creative person.[10] He was also a tough businessman, skilled in the practice of negotiation, and often crude and calculating in his struggle for power. It is perhaps easier for me to acknowledge his creative abilities now, eight years after his death. From this vantage, I can appreciate his entrepreneurial skills and life experiences and how they helped him to create this most original approach to American philanthropy.

Rod learned from his father the secret of peddling successful mail-order copy, which eventually made him wealthy in his own right, but he wanted more than that. After the Second World War he stayed in France, married a French woman, and tried to write the great American novel. However, his attempts were frustrated, and he felt his financial condition prevented him from becoming all that he could be. His wealthy father provided him with "a pittance," and the reporting jobs Rod took to make ends meet prevented him from devoting the time necessary for serious writing. Eventually, he gave up the manuscript, and returned with his family to the United States to work for his father. Although he did not discuss it, Rod was clearly frustrated, and even somewhat embarrassed, by his early failure at becoming an artist, which he blamed on his father.[11]

As an employee of his father's, Rod had some success, but saw no share in the profits until he created his own company in partnership with his father. As Rod told it, when that company began to be a success in 1975 his father attempted to take it away from him.[12] In reaction, Rod and his loyal employees staged a raid on the company, boxed up everything, and trucked it all away. Eventually, Rod reached a settlement with his father that left him at age fifty-five the sole owner of a company that overnight made him a millionaire.

Every year after that, until his death in 1984, Rod held a large party for his staff to celebrate the "breakaway." It was obvious that the breakaway was the most significant event of his career, and possibly of his life. It not only established him as independently wealthy, but also symbolized the final break from the domination and definition imposed by the relationship with his father.

Rod reveled in freedom. He supported First Amendment rights around the world, eventually creating his own foundation devoted to that cause.[13] For him, freedom meant not only the personal freedom to do as he wished, but also the right to say no to arbitrary power. For him, freedom of expression was absolute, or it was meaningless.

Although he was a lifelong liberal and champion of individual rights, specifically those of the downtrodden, he also fervently believed that his judgment—of cars, of wines, of books—would help set him apart, and give him a certain class or distinction others did not have. Perhaps Rod's most salient characteristic was his love of "the best." He believed that in any category—food, furnishings, travel—one could discover or create its most perfect exemplar. He enjoyed organizing tastings of wines, brandies, and beers (he loved to drink), and smoked hams and pâtés (he loved to eat), and to discover for himself (and for others) what was "the best."[14] We all enjoyed this quest of Rod's for the best, since it meant having a good time. The image I most associate with him is of the Spanish *compañero,* a word he admired both for its Romantic associations of loyalty and brotherhood and for its origins around food.

Rod lived passionately, with a great deal of energy and enthusiasm. He was unusually confident of himself and of his judgment on a broad range of interests. Because of his love of play, and his fierce and proud independence, he managed to both amuse and annoy just about every one of his friends and associates. He did not appear to care what others thought of him (although he was proud of being taken seriously by intellectuals). He enjoyed needling people, coming at them from unexpected directions, asking probing and often difficult questions. He was combative, and relished the fray. It is true that much of his sense of class was for show—he frequently mocked both himself and the pretensions he aspired to—but, like many people, he did seem to feel naturally superior to those who did not share his tastes, and was thrilled to have others he admired agree with him.

Whether it was conscious or not, Rod MacArthur invented the Fellows Program out of experiences from his own life, particularly events relating to his father. He believed that if he had been permitted to write his novel, he might have had the inner strength to define himself for himself, rather than in relation to his father. He saw the award as providing independence to people who were chomping at the bit, and giving them the opportunity for independence he did not have when he was young. The MacArthur Fellows Program became yet another manifestation of that celebration of personal freedom he felt in the breakaway from his father.[15]

Establishing the MacArthur Fellowship also fed Rod's appetite for belligerence and the struggle for power. While Rod and Bill Kirby vied for the leadership role in setting the agenda, Rod knew that getting there first with "his" program would make a big difference in setting the tone for the new Foundation, and in establishing his role in it. He was able to capitalize on the fact that Bill Kirby brought in Burch's article precisely because the two men were so-called enemies. By demonstrating goodwill in adopting Bill's suggestion, Rod thought he would have a beter chance of getting his own ideas across to the rest of the Board members if they appeared to be ideas previously endorsed by Kirby.

Finally, the MacArthur Fellowship fed Rod's desire to seek out the best. In one sense, the very opportunity of being on the Board of Directors and formulating the MacArthur Fellows Program allowed Rod to enjoy some of the best company in the world. Also, Rod served as chair of the selection committee and he relished the selection of Fellows—this experience was reminiscent of his delight in tasting fine wines and delicacies. Although we purposefully never attempted to determine who the best poets (or mathematicians) were, we did seek to identify the best candidates for this new award based on our criteria, and to make this program the best it could be.

3.

As we developed the MacArthur Fellows Program, we were aware of having to justify our actions and to exemplify certain values concerning creativity in at least four different areas: work, processes, groups, and individuals. We also wanted what we were creating to be original and valuable. Our conception of creativity in the Program was closely linked with the human attributes of curiosity: the love of exploration and discovery, a passion for making things, for seeing things anew, for tackling intractable problems, and the quest for growth, mastery, quality, and beauty. We designed this Program around the concept of unanticipated consequences.

The values that Rod and I envisioned for the Fellows Program included the celebration of the creative individual, the direct support of the creative process, and the sustaining of a creative environment. We deliberately avoided associating the Program with the values of finished products or commodities. Funding patterns that determine in advance what work would be supported placed a higher value on the end product than on the person doing the work, on the conditions, or on the processes of work itself. They represent a marketplace model of philanthropy. Directed research requires that there be a consensus in society, or at least between donor and recipient, regarding what might and should be done. These patterns are the product of a society that values commodities over individuals and their labor. They also imply a master/servant relationship in the support of human initiative and the advance of knowledge, where institutions define for individuals the nature and parameters of their work. It seemed to us that if institutions were structured around values associated with sustaining and supporting creative individuals, then the work within those institutions would ignite imaginations.

The kind of support we envisioned was the opposite of

directed research. We wanted this money to be entirely in the control of the recipients, who would be chosen for their creative abilities and their promise for achieving advances. No strings would be attached to how the money was used, and no reporting required—even though it was apparent that not every grant, nor every dollar, would be spent as effectively as it might on research or on behalf of society. We were willing to admit that normal grant programs, with applications devoted to projects, would stand a better chance of accomplishing various well-defined albeit limited objectives. The Program would not "take credit" for any breakthroughs or discoveries of those it supported, because the support was given directly to the individual without any kind of contract between the parties. We were willing to sever the customary connection between donor and product. By freeing creative individuals, through money that was personal to them, we would enable the recipients to plan for themselves what they would work on and how best to go about it.

Through our selections we would demonstrate models of creative individuals from different fields, ages, and professions. We came up with a set of traits for individuals that we felt would best characterize the type of person we sought. The traits we looked for included an internal motivation and drive to work (with or without sufficient support from us or anybody else); independence and originality of thought (Rod often used the term "mavericks"[16]); a thorough knowledge of subject matter (the capacity to move effectively beyond established norms); and a flexible approach to work (including the capacity to work in more than one discipline).

The traits we associate with creative individuals are most often projections of our ideals; the way we think of them can express our deepest-felt values. They include:

- Generosity of spirit and love of humanity[17]
- Openness to sensation and experience
- Aesthetic appreciation
- Empathy with other people and things
- Sense of humor

- Ability to play and work simultaneously
- Affinity for metaphor and how things may be connected[18]
- Sense of wonder
- Keenness of memory
- Acceptance of emotions
- Intuitive style
- Appreciation of and the ability to articulate the nature of freedom as the ultimate human condition
- Personal integrity and strength that can withstand and overcome pressures of conformity, arbitrary power, material success, and apathy
- Sense of quality, based on confidence and curiosity

The MacArthur Fellows Program would be more than just a way of bringing attention to the role of the independent artist/creator/investigator/researcher. Too often our society values trivialities, shoddy work, worthless notions, and pretentious ideas. We saw this Program as an expression of certain values related to individual excellence which ought to be given greater prominence in society. We hoped it would have implications for policy matters for other kinds of institutions, since we felt that it was essential for our culture to recognize and preserve the work of creative individuals generally, and to enhance their working conditions.

We hoped that business, industry, and education might also become more aware of the rich diversity of talents of those people working within their purview, and to encourage their individual development and expression. In every institution and profession there are people who are connoisseurs of individual talent and creativity. As Robert K. Merton has noted:

One has the impression that some people in almost every community have an eye for seeing talent of various kinds before this has become apparent to everyone else. Perhaps an effort should be made to search out these human counterparts to the truffle dog, these men and women who somehow see below the surface of appearance to underlying quality, who somehow know excellence when they first encounter it before others are cognizant

of it. Who are they? Some, no doubt, teachers who in the ordinary course of working at their job can't help being exposed
to youngsters. . . . [I]t could turn out that these informal spot-
ters of talent are found in many other walks of life as well. They
may be ministers or artists, newspaper editors or physicians.
The range of their occupations is probably wide, but they have
in common this eye for genuine ability of various kinds. They
are the unappointed talent scouts of America.[19]

For these reasons—to empower individuals, to stimulate institutions, and to benefit society—the Program had to succeed
on a number of levels, including with the public at large. We
saw this Program as placing a value on some of the important
ideas and the creative individuals that would help to define
our culture, now and in the future.

4.

Once the Board of Directors authorized the Fellows Program,
the nominators initated the process by proposing names, which
staff then developed for selection committee review. The core
of the Program resides in the activities of the selection committee. To operate successfully as a committee of strong individuals, it must be able to display creative processes in
coming together as a group, in reviewing the work of potential
candidates, and in making final selections through consensus.
We sought to create and over time we evolved a common set
of understandings that served as the basis for the committee's
deliberations. We also recognized that to operate effectively
the committee must each year reflect on itself and its decisions
with renewed self-awareness. The understandings or assumptions that express the values of the selection committee include:

- That individuals may express themselves creatively across
  a broad range of activities and skills
- That recognition and support of individuals and individual
  talents are important for society

- That values of society are demonstrated through reward mechanisms and incentives
- That such recognition helps to preserve cultural means and values
- That a diversity of thinking, ideologies, backgrounds, and aesthetics enhances the interaction of significant people
- That creative work is produced and creative individuals are found both within established institutions and in fringe groups and the avant-garde
- That an openness to cultural stimuli from a diverse, even divergent, spectrum is important to enhance creativity
- That personal power derives from exercising craftsmanship and striving for mastery
- That there is a higher value on becoming than on being[20]

The operations of the committee are spare, the discussions are rich, and the workload is heavy. The committee is composed of around twelve experts chosen from different disciplines, backgrounds, and interests. Every year a few selectors leave and others are added. The committee meets eight times per year in all-day meetings to review files of nominees. There are no subcommittees by discipline, and all the selectors review all of the same files. Their decisions are integral to the developing (or discarding) of files on nominees, as they interpret the selection criteria through the vetting of nominations. Once a year at the final meeting they make the selections of MacArthur Fellows.

The mandate of the selection committee is to review the many creative nominations and to pick the ones that best meet the established criteria. Each file is unique, bringing with it criteria of judgment particular to its own field, and each is subjected to a thorough scrutiny, based on what evidence is available. Most files contain conflicting points of view. Consideration of the three award criteria against the bulky paper files sifts out needed facts: what can be learned about the person, the work, and the difference a MacArthur Fellowship might make.

The first task of selectors is to create in their minds a characterization of the real persons brought out in the files. The staff and the committee do not interview candidates. The selectors bring to the table their own values and sense of an ideal creative type, based on their life experiences and professional qualifications. They review the reference letters from the files, which are attempts by yet others to characterize the individual and offer advice.

The advice we recieve, in the form of nominations and reference letters, concerns how each correspondent views the individual under consideration and the Fellows Program itself. This advice also derives from a sense of their ideals and values. The many interpretations of the Program involve different views of creativity and of the roles of creative individuals in society. In this sense the Program may be compared with the fable of the blind men and the elephant. Each person sees a different aspect of something momentous. Some see the MacArthur Fellowship as an award for past achievement, some as a fellowship for future promise; some want it to go to senior practitioners in their fields, others to younger and less-recognized persons; some agree with the premises of the Program, others feel that awards should be made for specific projects, or be targeted to specific fields, or provide less money or time. The advice from references, then, concerns many things, including what the referee would like to see happen; what they feel is in the best interests of the nominee, the field or profession, and the Program itself; and what they feel is the right thing to do.[21]

A dynamic emerges in the selection committee from the interrelationships between the creative individual portrayed by the paper file and the constructs in the minds of selectors (which are balanced against various forms of ideal types). All of this is an attempt to get as close as possible to the actual person. As the selection process moves to completion, the fate of each file is determined by the mix of these disparate elements, and by the capacity of each file to define the person it represents as accurately as possible in terms of the operating criteria.

Candidates are reviewed over a period of time—anywhere

from one year to several. This gives selectors the opportunity to reflect on the issues without having to make choices against a deadline. This flexible time scheme allows each selector to prepare for the meetings by reading the comments of others in the files, reviewing the work of the nominees, sharing thoughts, and hearing those of others on the committee. The time between meetings serves as an incubation period. The process is iterative, and is marked by deep and careful readings which selectors do in alternating sequences—at home alone, then tested with the group, then at home again, and so forth throughout the year. This builds toward a momentum of decision-making within the group.[22] Each time the files resurface they have been augmented by new material; most files are seen a minimum of three times before final selections are made.

The meetings of the selection committee assume different styles and shapes depending on the files under consideration. These styles range from book clubs and art seminars to scientific colloquia, political forums, community groups, and so forth. Selectors view the work of nominees as an indication of their creativity and promise. They regard such work— books, paintings, scientific articles, pieces of music, effective community action—as maps of creativity.[23] Selectors chart their course through the year by a careful review of nominees' work, in which they search for clues. One selector remarked that the selection experience was like "taking a graduate seminar in everything."

How can a selection committee of limited numbers adequately and fairly evaluate individuals from such a broad range of fields and activities?[24] Much of it has to do with a developed understanding of various forms of rhetoric. One learns, in almost any profession, to read letters of reference with a critical eye. Wayne Booth discusses three levels of rhetoric associated with making judgments.[25] The first concerns expert knowledge within a discipline—what we expect practitioners to know and care about (peer review). The second consists of general and tacit assumptions about values which we all use in making judgments, including how the past might predict the future and what value we place on certain kinds of work.

The third level, which Booth calls the "rhetoric of inquiry, or of intellectual engagement," lies between the specificity of the first and the generality of the second. As he writes,

> We learn how to judge whether the arguments in fields beyond our full competence *somehow* track, whether the style of presentation somehow accords with standards we recognize. We learn to sense whether a colleague, even in a quite remote field, *seems* to have mastered the tricks of the trade—not just the trade of this or that kind of economist or philosopher, but the tricks of this whole trade, the trade of learning and teaching for the sake of learning and teaching.[26]

For the selectors, then, who must consider what Booth calls "this whole trade" in a larger context than the academic one of which Booth speaks, their concern is how each individual meets certain culturally defined standards of quality within society at large.

Selectors review hundreds of files on creative individuals based on hundreds of different conceptions. The judgment of selectors derives from reviewing a broad array of evidence and weighing each piece carefully with respect to the operating criteria. Some view creativity on the basis of a certain lifestyle, usually nonconformist, authentic, imaginative. Robert Root-Berstein writes (concerning eccentric lifestyles), "Your probability of discovering or inventing something different increases as your experiences, hobbies, skills, knowledge, philosophy, and goals become increasingly unusual."[27] Creativity may also be evaluated on the basis of performance, in which certain standards are expected to be met within the particular discipline. A third view of creative individuals concerns those who "produce something of cultural value."[28] Our focus is on creative individuals of all kinds, especially those who are able to define themselves through their works, and by these definitions explain something about mastery of craftsmanship, growth, and human potential.[29]

5.

The MacArthur Foundation is the direct result of John D. MacArthur's creation of wealth and the bequest in his will. He knew what he did best—make money—and he deliberately designated to others the task of how to spend it. With the MacArthur Fellows Program, we have in some ways imitated that bequest. While the donor gave his money to a foundation, we proceeded to give it to creative individuals. As with the original bequest, no strings are attached. How the money is used is left to those receiving the gift, who become responsible for it.

In essence, the MacArthur Fellows Program is about gifts and gift-giving. The intention of the gift is to unlock the unlimited powers of the imagination. As Lewis Hyde has written:

> Whatever is given is supposed to be given away again, not kept. Or, if it is kept, something of similar value should move on in its stead, the way a billiard ball may stop when it sends another scurrying across the felt, its momentum transferred. You may keep your Christmas present, but it ceases to be a gift in the true sense unless you have given something else away. As it is passed along, the gift may be given back to the original donor, but this is not essential. In fact, it is better if the gift is not returned but is given instead to some new, third party. The only essential is this: the gift must always move. There are other forms of property that stand still, that mark a boundary or resist momentum, but the gift keeps going.[30]

For some, the MacArthur Fellowship has become a cultural symbol of excellence. If so, the most important element of that symbol is its diversity—its demonstration of creativity from scholarship to activism, from the arts to the sciences, from the laboratories to the streets—all focused on individuals rather than on institutions, and in every case providing freedom from constraints.

As I have said, we designed this Program with unanticipated consequences in mind. Each year we reinvented the idea by testing the criteria established by the Board against the nominations we received. We were deliberately searching for and working out a method that would utilize ambiguity tolerance as a tool to admit many models in one program. For some, the ambiguity may prove intolerant, but most people recognize the Fellows Program as an investment in individuals over the long term. Through this Program we have tried to demonstrate the variety of ways in which creativity and creative thinking can be applied to philanthropy. To the extent that we have achieved this end, it has been by making the Program as human as possible. It may mean that flaws seep into the process, but as with every human process, there are also sparks.

NOTES

1. I am grateful to Mirdza Berzins for reviewing and editing this manuscript with me.
2. The five-year stipend, which depends entirely on the age of the recipient, is currently set at \$150,000 to \$375,000. The scale begins at age twenty-one with \$30,000 for the first year, to which \$1,000 annual increments are added until age sixty-six. It is subject to taxation.
3. A great many people were critically involved in developing the Fellows Program, including most of the MacArthur Foundation Board members at the time—William Kirby, Robert Ewing, Paul Doolen—and, later, Murray Gell-Mann, Jonas Salk, Jerome Wiesner, Jack Corbally, and Edward Levi. The first program director was Gerald Freund. This essay concerns Rod MacArthur, but in no way is meant to minimize the contributions of others.
4. Among the books consulted for this paper are included Rollo May, *The Courage to Create* (New York: W. W. Norton & Co. Inc., 1975); John A. Glover, Royce R. Ronnig, & Cecil R. Reynolds (Eds.), *Handbook of Creativity* (New York: Plenum Press, 1989); Silvano Arieti, *Creativity: The Magic Synthesis* (New York: Basic Books, 1976); R. Ochse, *Before the Gates of Excellence: The Determinants of Creative Genius* (New York: Cambridge University Press, 1990); Elisabeth Young-Bruehl, *Creative Characters* (New York: Routledge, 1991); Robert Scott Root-Bernstein,

Discovering: Inventing and Solving Problems at the Frontiers of Scientific Knowledge (Cambridge, MA: Harvard University Press, 1989). I am especially grateful for two books by Robert Grudin, *Time and the Art of Living* (New York: Ticknor & Fields, 1982) and *The Grace of Great Things: Creativity and Innovation* (New York: Ticknor & Fields, 1990). I also absorbed much from my experience at the MacArthur Foundation.

5. Robert K. Merton, " 'Recognition' and 'Excellence': Instructive Ambiguities" (1960) in his *The Sociology of Science: Theoretical and Empirical Investigations,* edited by Norman W. Storer (Chicago: University of Chicago Press, 1973), pp. 419–438. Merton served as an early adviser to the Program.

6. Plato, *The Republic* (Modern Library, 1982), translated by Benjamin Jowett, p. 7.

7. George Burch, "Of Venture Research," *The American Heart Journal* (December 1976).

8. See Leigh Van Valen, "Dishonesty and Grants," *Nature,* 1976; Daniel S. Greenberg, "Longshot Research," *The Washington Post,* 1977; Bruce L. R. Smith & Joseph J. Karlesky, *The State of Academic Science: The Universities in the Nation's Research Effort* (New Rochelle, NY: Change Magazine Press, 1977); Ludwig Fleck, *Genesis and Development of a Scientific Fact* (Chicago: University of Chicago Press, 1979); and Kenneth Hope, "The MacArthur Fellows Program: Some Frequently Asked Questions" (1987), program document for the John D. and Catherine T. MacArthur Foundation.

9. Rod MacArthur used to ask how people would know what they were going to discover until they found it. In his article "The Encouragement of Science" (*Scientific American,* 1968, pp. 170–178), Warren Weaver reported that a scientist on the board of the Rockefeller Foundation explained to another trustee about a potential grant recipient: "If he knew just what he was going to do, he wouldn't need to do it." (Quoted in Root-Bernstein, *Discovering,* p. 407.)

10. A passage from F. Barron and D. M. Harrington in "Creativity, Intelligence, and Personality" (*Annual Review of Psychology,* 1981, p. 453) summarizes many years of research on the personalities of creative individuals. It seems to me a fairly accurate description of Rod MacArthur's personality: "High valuation of esthetic qualities in experience, broad interests, attraction to complexity, high energy, independence of judgement, auton-

omy, intuition, self-confidence, ability to resolve or accom-
modate apparently opposite or conflicting traits in one's self
concept, and finally, a firm sense of self as 'creative.' "

11. I am not arguing that this was the case, only that Rod thought
so.

12. William Kirby vigorously disputed Rod's version of events concerning the breakaway.

13. The J. Roderick MacArthur Foundation in Niles, IL.

14. I shared Rod's love of food and drink, but used to argue about
the concept of "the best." In many respects a Platonist, he believed there were rules which defined the best in every category
of thing or experience. All one had to do was to understand and
recognize the logic of those rules. Since I was more of a relativist
when it came to discussions of "the best," he would accuse me
of not believing in rules at all. I agreed that there were a great
many rules, but that many of them were mutually contradictory.
He thought I was being difficult.

15. Rod created reunions (yearly gatherings) for recipients of the
MacArthur Fellowship, which are extended celebrations of the
freedom of the Fellowship. The reunions are reminiscent of
the "breakaway" parties he held.

16. Rod had a great deal of sympathy for outsiders, those who are
defined by the difference between themselves and the collectiv-
ity. For this, see Georg Simmel, "The Stranger," in *The Sociology
of Georg Simmel,* edited and translated by Kurt H. Wolff (New
York: The Free Press, 1950), pp. 402–408; Robert Ezra Park,
"Human Migration and the Marginal Man," in his *Race and
Culture* (New York: The Free Press, 1950), pp. 345–356; Everett
Stonequist, *The Marginal Man* (New York: Scribners, 1937);
Alfred Schutz, "The Stranger," in his *Collected Papers II,* edited
by Arvid Brodersen (The Hague: Martinus Nijhoff, 1964), pp.
91–105; and Charles Axelrod, *Studies in Intellectual Breakthrough:
Freud, Simmel, Buber* (Amherst, MA: University of Massachu-
setts Press, 1979), which was my source for the other references.

17. Of course, creative people can be just as swinish as anyone else.

18. "All things are interwoven with one another; a sacred bond
unites them; there is scarcely one thing that is isolated from
another," Marcus Aurelius, *Meditations,* translated by Maxwell
Staniforth (New York: Penguin Books, 1964), p. 106.

19. See Merton, " 'Recognition' and 'Excellence,' " p. 426.

20. This list owes some of its constructions to Robert S. Lynd,

Knowledge for What? The Place of Social Science in American Culture (Princeton, NJ: Princeton University Press, 1967), pp. 192–197; and to Arieti, *Creativity,* pp. 312–325.

21. For more on this topic, see Nicholas Rescher, "Good Advice," in *Human Interests: Reflections on Philosophical Anthropology* (Stanford, CA: Stanford University Press, 1990), pp. 22–35.

22. These stages resemble in some ways the model of creative process put forth by G. Wallas, *The Act of Thought* (New York: Watts, 1926). We did not, of course, pattern the selection process after Wallas.

23. I believe, as do many others, that one can learn more about creativity through experiencing original works than by reading psychologists or others on creativity. In this regard, I find the following remarks especially noteworthy. Adam Smith, in *Of the Imitative Arts* (1777), wrote, "The Nobler Works of Statuary and Painting appear to us a sort of wonderful phaenomena, differing in this respect from the wonderful phaenomena of Nature, that they carry, as it were, their own explication along with them, and demonstrate, even to the eye, the way and manner in which they were produced." Also see Axelrod, *Intellectual Breakthrough,* p. 1: "To recall a product of intellectual breakthrough while forgetting the analytic conditions of its utterance is to have the answer but no memory of the question."

24. As La Rochefoucauld said, "Everybody complains about his memory; nobody complains about his judgement."

25. Wayne C. Booth, "The Idea of a Uni-versity: As Viewed by a Rhetorician" (Ryerson Lecture, University of Chicago, 1967).

26. Ibid.

27. Root-Bernstein, *Discovering,* p. 409.

28. R. Ochse, *Before the Gates of Excellence,* p. 3.

29. One component of these criteria—that the award should make a difference to the individual—has led the committee to turn down some of the best and most creative persons. One Board member, who claims to find this result both absurd and amusing, labels such persons "Too Good." There have been a great many of them.

30. Lewis Hyde, *The Gift* (New York: Vintage Books, 1979), p. 4.

INVENTING THE UNIVERSE

RICHARD MORRIS

EVERYONE KNOWS HOW SCIENCE IS SUPPOSED TO WORK

Everyone knows how science is supposed to work. First you make a hypothesis. It may be a good one or a bad one. But you need a hypothesis. Then you use your idea to deduce certain expected experimental results. When the experiments are performed, either your idea is confirmed or it is shot out of the water. If you're lucky enough to have guessed right, and if a second team of experimenters succeeds in replicating the results, your hypothesis is well on its way to becoming an accepted theory.

Of course this is an oversimplified account. Matters are rarely so straightforward. Experimental results are frequently ambiguous, and scientists often engage in a lot of debate before they profess themselves willing to accept a new idea. But I think that the majority of scientists would agree that the outline I have given is a resonably accurate description of the way that science works most of the time.

In others words, it's a pretty good description of ordinary, everyday science, the kind that most scientists spend their lives doing. On the other hand, this paradigm totally fails to describe the really important scientific discoveries, the ones that transform our conception of the universe. Everyday science may be done in a reasonably logical, straightforward way. However, those great bursts of scientific creativity that change our ideas about the nature of things typically fail to conform to the usual pattern. Scientific discovery is as illogical and unpredictable as creative activity in any of the arts. The creators of great new scientific insight depend as much on intuition and unarticulated feeling as any creative artist. And when their insights become known in the scientific community, they often seem so dazzling that they are accepted long before they are conclusively confirmed by empirical evidence. In fact, the great ideas in science sometimes flourish even when they are confronted with evidence that seems to contradict them.

DARWIN, GALILEO

It is not hard to find examples. For example, Charles Darwin knew nothing of the mechanisms of genetic inheritance. The modern theory of genetics was a creation of the twentieth century, and Darwin died in 1882. Consequently, when Darwin's critics charged that natural selection could not possibly operate the way Darwin claimed it did, he could not answer them. The best he could do was to fall back on an absurd theory of inheritance called pangenesis.

When Darwin's ideas about pangenesis could not be confirmed, he should have given up his ideas about natural selection. Or at least he should have admitted that they now seemed somewhat doubtful. But of course Darwin did nothing of the sort. He continued to insist on the validity of his ideas, and the theory of evolution quickly triumphed. By the end of the century, evolutionary ideas were generally accepted among biologists.

Both Darwin and Galileo were attacked on religious grounds. Unfortunately, Galileo lived in an earlier era, when the Church was much more powerful. But he was so convinced of the importance and correctness of Copernicus's idea that the planets revolved around the sun that he rushed headlong into a confrontation with the Inquisition. In the end, Galileo was threatened with torture and forced to recant his ideas. His writings were condemned, and he was placed under house arrest for the remainder of his life.

And did Galileo have proof of the theory for which he risked so much? Of course not. In fact, direct empirical proof of the rotation of the earth was not obtained until 1851, some 209 years after Galileo's death. To be sure, Galileo had constructed a telescope, and had discovered mountains on the moon and four satellites of Jupiter. But these discoveries did nothing to support the Copernican hypothesis. At best, they only discredited some of the old Aristotelian ideas about the perfectibility of the cosmos. The fact that a planet possesses moons, after all, has no implications for the question of whether it revolves around the sun or the earth.

Galileo knew that Copernicus had been right. But he couldn't prove it. So, in the end, he did what Darwin was later to do. He fell back on a questionable theory. One of the arguments—in fact, it was supposed to be the clinching argument—that Galileo advanced in support of the heliocentric hypothesis was his own, rather convoluted, theory of ocean tides. According to Galileo, the motion of the earth caused the seas to slosh back and forth in their basins. It was this that caused the sea level to rise and fall according to certain patterns. Not only was this idea incorrect (the tides are caused by the gravitational attractions of the sun and moon), it was contradicted by Galileo's own theories of motion. He should have known that the oceans would simply move along with the earth as it rotated, as everything else on our planet's surface did.

The idea that the planets revolved around the sun was not Galileo's. But Galileo was certainly the theory's most persistent advocate. By promulgating Copernicus's theory, he paved the way for later scientists, such as Johannes Kepler and Isaac Newton, who worked out ideas about planetary motion in greater detail, and made the heliocentric hypothesis irrefutable in the process. Galileo richly deserves the exalted position he has been given in the history of science, as much for his advocacy of Copernicus's theory as for his own discoveries.

But when we look at Galileo's work, we find that it fails to conform to any commonly accepted ideas about the way in which science is supposed to be conducted. Galileo was not one to discard a hypothesis when he found that there was no adequate proof for it—not if he really believed it to be true. In fact, we now know that Galileo went so far as to fake some of his experimental results. If he knew how an experiment *should* turn out, he described it that way whether it had worked that way in the laboratory or not. In the case of Copernicus's heliocentric hypothesis, Galileo would scrape up whatever evidence he could find in support of the theory, whether that evidence was very good or not. Galileo knew he was right, and he would do anything he could to convince others of that fact.

FOUCAULT'S PENDULUM

In 1851, the French physicist Jean Foucault performed an experiment with a large, heavy pendulum. He found that the direction in which the pendulum swung back and forth gradually shifted as the earth rotated under it. Finally, there was experimental proof that the earth really moved.

It is unlikely that the experiment swayed any skeptics, however. The only doubters of the heliocentric theory who remained were the crackpots. Galileo and his successors had simply been too convincing. Their vision had been so profound and compelling that the idea of a sun-centered solar system had been generally accepted for at least two centuries by this time. Empirical proofs had been slow in coming. However, everyone had been able to see that the heliocentric theory *worked*.

MODERN SCIENCE

Scientific fashions may change. Theories may be discredited and other theories invented to take their place. But there is one thing that remains the same. In modern times, one still finds great innovative scientists insisting on the correctness of ideas for which they have little or no proof. And their theories are often accepted before there is much empirical evidence to support them. Sometimes it is vision, not evidence, that counts.

For example, Einstein's theory of gravitation, his general theory of relativity, was accepted by scientists long before there was much evidence to support it. Although Einstein propounded his theory in 1915, it wasn't until the 1960s that accurate experimental tests of it were performed. And by this time, the theory had functioned as a foundation for all serious speculation in cosmology for decades.

To be sure, the British astronomer Arthur Eddington had performed a famous empirical test of the theory in 1919. Einstein had pointed out that his theory implied that a ray of starlight that grazed the surface of the sun would not travel in a straight line. On the contrary, its trajectory would be bent. In 1919, Eddington had made observations of starlight passing by the sun during a total eclipse, and had reported that Einstein's predictions had turned out to be correct. However, the "proof" really wasn't as convincing as many scientists claimed. The observations had been difficult and the margin of error had been large. One could just as easily have argued that the question of the validity of Einstein's theory was still open. In the end, scientists believed because they wanted to believe.

One can argue the issue of how convincing Eddington's confirmation of Einstein's theory should have been. On the other hand, there really isn't much room for debate about confirmations of the inflationary universe theory of MIT physicist Alan Guth. Today, this is the most important theory in the field of cosmology. And yet, not only is Guth's theory unsupported by any empirical evidence, the only testable prediction that it has yielded has turned out to be false. Yet the theory explains so much, and gives so compelling an explanation of certain obvious features of the universe, that few scientists doubt its validity. I will have more to say about Guth's theory later. For now, I will confine myself to noting that this is another case where vision and explanatory power have turned out to be more important than experimental "proof."

Another theory that is unsupported by any direct evidence is one propounded by the British physicist Stephen Hawking. One of Hawking's best-known theories has to do with so-called mini black holes. According to Hawking, such objects could have been formed early in the history of the universe. If they were, he says, they could exhibit a kind of behavior which is entirely different than that of ordinary black holes, which are the collapsed remnants of dead suns.

An ordinary black hole, physicists agree, can only increase in mass with time. This follows from the fact that a black hole is an object in which gravitational fields are so strong that nothing, not even rays of light, can escape from them. Any matter that strays into the vicinity of a black hole will eventually be sucked into the dark object. And any mass that does enter a black hole will remain there until the end of time.

On the other hand, according to Hawking's theoretical analysis, a very small black hole, one weighing less than about a billion tons (by comparison, our sun, which is an average-sized star, weighs about 2.2 million billion trillion tons), can spontaneously lose mass, and finally explode in a burst of light.

No one seriously doubts this theory. However, it has never had empirical confirmation of any kind. Not only has no one ever seen a mini black hole explode, it has not even been established that they exist. It is entirely possible that these mini black hole explosions exist nowhere but in the mind of Stephen Hawking.

EINSTEIN

It would be impossible to discuss the role played by creative imagination in science without taking a long look at the work of Albert Einstein. After all, few would dispute the contention that he was the greatest physicist of the twentieth century. His special and general theories of relativity provide the foundation for much of modern physics, and he also made significant contributions to the development of quantum mechanics, the other great modern theory.

Even when Einstein went astray, he did so in a grandiose way. For example, he spent his later years fruitlessly seeking a unified field theory, a theory that would give a comprehensive explanation of all of the known forces of nature. In doing so, Einstein isolated himself from his colleagues, who generally thought that he was wasting his time. To be sure, Einstein did not succeed in the quest. However, his efforts now seem less quixotic than they appeared at the time. For today, scientists are again seeking a theory that will unify all the forces. Indeed, some of them believe that superstring theory (a topic that I will discuss later) will turn out to be such a "theory of everything."

Many of the scientific ideas that Einstein proposed were novel and surprising. He must have been conscious of the fact that some of them would not achieve wide acceptance until they were subjected to experimental test. In fact. Einstein often suggested possible experiments himself. His papers on the special theory of relativity in 1905 and on the general theory in 1915 suggest experimental tests that might be possible.

But when the experiments were actually performed, Einstein often behaved with surprising indifference. For example, in 1905, he had pointed out that the special theory of relativity implied that the mass of a body should increase when it was accelerated to velocities approaching the speed of light.

Even today we cannot make macroscopic bodies travel that fast. For example, the most rapidly moving space vehicles travel at much less than light velocity. However, Einstein's theory is just as applicable to the behavior of subatomic particles as it is to that of large objects. An electron, for example, becomes much heavier when it moves at velocities approaching that of light.

In 1906, one year after Einstein's theory was published, the German physicist Walter Kaufman published the results of a long series of experiments in which he had measured the mass of moving electrons. Kaufman found that his results agreed with some theories and disagreed with others. In particular, they seemed to contradict the predictions of Einstein's theory. There was a small but significant difference between Kaufman's findings and calculations based on the special theory of relativity.

Einstein hardly seemed troubled at all. Commenting on the two competing theories that Kaufman's experiments seemed to support, he wrote, "In my opinion both theories have a rather small probability because their fundamental assumptions concerning the mass of moving electrons are not explainable in terms of theoretical systems which embrace a greater complex of phenomena."

In other words, no matter what the experiments said, the competing theories could not be true because they did not fit into far-reaching theoretical patterns. In Einstein's eyes, the reach and logical structure of a theory could be more important than results that were obtained in the laboratory. Like the ancient Greek philosophers, Einstein believed that creative thought alone could grasp the structure of reality. If experiment contradicted such a vision, then so much the worse for experiment.

Thus we should not be surprised to discover that Einstein should have behaved in a similar manner when one of his theories appeared to have been confirmed. When Eddington's measurements of starlight in 1919 appeared to confirm the general theory, this fact was reported in newspapers around the world. But when Einstein heard of Eddington's results, he seemed relatively unmoved. This prompted one of his students, Ilse Rosenthal-Schneider, to ask him why he wasn't as excited as she was. Einstein replied, "But I knew that the theory is correct." When Rosenthal-Schneider asked him how he would have reacted if Eddington had gotten results contradicting the theory, he answered, "Then I would have been sorry for the dear Lord—the theory is correct."

While he was still an adolescent, Einstein had lost his religious faith. Yet as an adult he frequently spoke of "God" or of the "good Lord" when discussing scientific theory. When he did this, he was making utterances such as one might expect from a mystic. It was as though he equated seeing into the mind of God with discovering the underlying order of the universe.

I am not suggesting that Einstein was a mystic, or that mystical insights can yield information about the physical universe (and I'll pass over the question of whether they yield information about anything else). In any case, Einstein's discoveries certainly weren't the result of meditation. They were the product of concentrated thought about scientific problems. What I would suggest is that the creative imagination of an Einstein often appears to have certain magical qualities, so that it seems perfectly natural to speak in such terms. Einstein's insights were not those of a mystic, or of a poet or artist. But his imagination worked in similar ways. It may be significant that Beethoven sometimes spoke as though he could see into the mind of God too, when he was writing his music.

Insights are not always correct, and there were times when Einstein was terribly mistaken. Yet, even when he was wrong, he sometimes made significant contributions to physics. For example, Einstein consistently refused to accept the interpretations of quantum mechanics (the theory which describes the behavior of atoms and subatomic particles) developed by the Danish physicist Niels Bohr and his colleagues at Bohr's institute for theoretical physics in Copenhagen. Einstein's objections seem wrongheaded to us today. In fact, it has been proved that the kind of theory Einstein claimed would eventually replace quantum mechanics is impossible. Yet the discussions and arguments that he and Bohr had over the years did a great deal to clarify physicists' ideas about the theory. Even when Einstein was wrong, he added to our understanding of the universe.

THE INFLATIONARY UNIVERSE

Sometimes a theory can win general acceptance even when the only empirical evidence that has been obtained contradicts it. Such is the case concerning one of the ideas I have mentioned previously, the inflationary universe theory. In its original form, this theory, which Guth proposed in 1980, made just one testable prediction. This prediction was contradicted by observation. But this did not cause the theory to be discarded. It was simply modified to avoid the difficulty. Today, Guth's theory has gained nearly universal acceptance among astronomers and cosmologists.

According to Guth, the universe underwent a very rapid "inflationary" expansion early in its history. Guth suggests that when the universe was about 10^{-35} seconds* old (that is, 10^{-35} seconds after the big bang), a kind of antigravitational force permeated the universe, causing it to expand at an extremely rapid rate for a brief period of time.

This assumption, by the way, is not as gratuitous as it might seem. There are good reasons for believing that, under the extreme conditions that existed in the very early universe, such a force could have indeed existed. Some of the theories on which Guth based his original idea are quite speculative. However, the idea of an inflationary expansion is not intrinsically unreasonable.

By the time the universe was about 10^{-32} seconds old, Guth says, the inflationary phase was over. At this point, the universe settled down and continued to expand at the more leisurely pace that we observe today. Though inflation continued for only a brief period, he says, the effects were dramatic. The universe could have increased in size by a factor of 10^{50} or more during this interval.

What we have here is a theory that proposes that something very extraordinary went on at a time many billions of years in the past. It happened so long ago that we cannot possibly observe it.

The original version of Guth's theory predicted that the inflationary expansion should have taken place in a lot of separate domains, or spatial bubbles. As these domains expanded, they would have come into contact with one another, coa-

*The number 10^{35} is represented by the number "1" followed by 35 zeros; 10^{-35} is 1 divided by 10^{35}. Thus 10^{-35} is a very small number.

lescing into one big universe. In other words, according to the theory, the universe should have the appearance of a mass of soap bubbles.

Obviously, there was something wrong with this. Astronomers know very well that the universe doesn't have this kind of appearance. Fortunately, the difficulty was soon solved. Other physicists worked out versions of the theory in which this problem was avoided. It was shown that the "soap bubbles" would be so much larger than the observable universe that they would not be observed. Guth's theory was well on the way to success.

WHY?

Why was the inflationary universe successful if it was unsupported by any new evidence? Because it was a clear, logical theory that seemed to explain many puzzling features of the universe with which other theories had been unable to come to terms. It was as though scientists were looking at Guth's ideas and saying, "Of course! There had to have been an inflationary expansion. If there hadn't been, things wouldn't look the way they do now."

Space limitations prevent me from describing in detail the features of the present-day universe that the inflationary theory explains. In any case, there are numerous books which discuss the inflationary scenario in detail, and which also explain other important ideas in cosmology. The only point that I want to make here is that an imaginative idea can be widely accepted in the absence of any direct empirical confirmation if it makes other scientific knowledge cohere in an elegant, logical way.

THE CREATIVE IMAGINATION RUNS RAMPANT

Einstein's theories were eventually confirmed by laboratory experiments. Guth's theory has not been. Indeed, it may never be possible to test it, not unless someone can find a way to travel back in time and observe the events that took place a tiny fraction of a second after the big bang. However, there is a significant connection between Guth's theory and observable reality; scientists are convinced that a period of inflationary expansion—or something like it—is necessary if the kind of universe we observe today is to be created.

But one should not assume that such connections between theory and reality always exist. In some cases they do not. For example, the British physicist Stephen Hawking is notorious for concocting theoretical ideas which are quite appealing to the scientific mind, but which don't seem to have much relevance to anything that can actually be seen.

When I say this, it is not my intention to denigrate Hawking's achievement. On the contrary, I would point out that he possesses one of the truly creative scientific intellects of our time. And because he does, his thought sometimes ranges far from anything that can be observed.

Much of Hawking's earlier work dealt with black holes. For example, there was the theoretical analysis of the behavior of mini black holes that I mentioned previously. During the 1960s, in collaboration with the British physicist Roger Penrose, Hawking also proved some theorems dealing with the behavior of matter inside black holes. In particular, Hawking and Penrose showed that matter that enters a black hole must eventually become concentrated in a region of zero volume in the hole's interior called a singularity. Or at least this will be the case if the assumptions with which Hawking and Penrose began are correct.

In order to prove their result, Hawking and Penrose made the assumption that Einstein's theory of general relativity continued to be valid under the most extreme conditions. In reality, there are good reasons for believing that this is not the case. Every theory has its limits, even those as well confirmed as Einstein's. But then the two British scientists were only engaging in a theoretical exercise, not trying to predict something that could actually be observed, so there is really no reason to criticize them.

The reason that a singularity (if singularities really exist) could never be observed is that nothing ever gets out of a black hole. It is impossible to see what is going on inside a black hole because, if we try to shine a ray of light into it, the light ray is captured; it remains inside the hole forever. Nor can we observe the interior of a black hole by any other means. Nothing—not light, not particles, not any kind of radiation—can ever get out of it to provide us with any information.

It can be argued that the Hawking–Penrose theorems increase our understanding of the universe even though they yield no testable predictions. They do elucidate the logical structure of gravitational theory, after all, and tell us something about what black holes should theoretically be like. There does seem to be good evidence that these condensed, dark objects really do exist, and one would like to have some kind of an idea of what is going on inside a black hole even if the events that take place in that region cannot be seen.

IMAGINARY TIME

As the years have passed, some of Hawking's work has come to seem less and less relevant to the observable world. For example, in his book *A Brief History of Time,* Hawking expounds a theory which he developed in collaboration with the American physicist James B. Hartle. According to this theory, the universe may exist for a finite period of time, and yet have neither a beginning nor an end.

The early universe, Hawking and Hartle say, may have existed in imaginary time. Now "imaginary time" sounds like a very mysterious, perhaps even poetic, concept. However, when Hawking and his collaborator use this term, what they have in mind is something that is really very straightforward. When they speak of imaginary time, they mean that, in the early universe, time may bear greater resemblance to a spatial dimension than it does to the quantity we observe today. In other words, it is possible that the early universe didn't really exist in time at all, that it was an object which possessed only spatial or spacelike dimensions.

Today, we live in a four-dimensional world. There are three dimensions of space and one dimension of time. There isn't anything very mysterious about time's status as a "dimension," by the way. When we say this we only mean that four coordinates are required to specify where an event takes place. It does us little good, for example, to know that a plane will leave a particular airport in New York if we don't also know the time of departure.

In the hypothetical universe envisioned by Hawking and Hartle, matters are somewhat different. If we go back far enough in time, then time ceases to have this character. It becomes a spacelike dimension instead. The universe of Hawking and Hartle, then, resembles a four-dimensional sphere. If something like this can really happen, then there is no beginning. An analogy is provided by the earth, which is a three-dimensional sphere. Obviously, the surface of the earth does not "begin" or "end" anywhere. According to Hawking and Hartle, the universe could have the same character.

If the universe "begins" in such a manner, it could have a similar "end." Although the universe is expanding now, it does not necessarily follow that it will expand forever. Gravitational forces are slowing the expansion. If they are powerful enough (and no one really knows whether or not they are), they may eventually cause the expansion to stop. If this happens, a phase of contraction will set in. If the universe does ever begin to contract, then gravity will cause the contraction to continue at an ever-increasing pace. After billions of years, the entire universe will be compressed into a small volume, and conditions similar to those that existed at the beginning will be re-created. Scientists sometimes speak of such an event as a "big crunch," in analogy with the big bang.

In the Hawking–Hartle theory, however, the big crunch does not really cause the universe to come to an end. Instead, the time dimension regains its "imaginary" character, and again becomes spacelike. Once again there is a four-dimensional sphere. Just as there was no beginning, there is also no end.

OTHER UNIVERSES

The imaginary time theory is described in Hawking's book. But of course he didn't stop doing theoretical work in physics when he completed the manuscript. He has since gone on to do work that has an even more startling character. For example, Hawking has suggested that all of the subatomic particles that scientists observe might originally have come from other universes.

According to Hawking's hypothesis, our universe is connected to other universes by numerous microscopic wormholes. The idea of a wormhole, incidentally, is not original with Hawking. It is a concept that has some foundation in Einstein's general theory of relativity. One can think of a wormhole as a passageway that connects two widely separated regions of space. These regions can be two places within our own universe. If other universes exist, wormholes could connect them.

According to Hawking, subatomic particles may constantly traverse such wormholes, and pass from one universe to another. These wormholes would not be observable. If they exist, they would be so small that they could not be seen. And of course, the universes from which they arrived and into which they escaped could not be detected either (if they could be, they wouldn't be alternate universes). Nor can one ever see particles disappear or suddenly pop into existence, if Hawking's ideas are correct. In his theory, everything is arranged so that, whenever a particle of our universe disappears, an identical particle appears from elsewhere to take its place.

In other words, at first glance, the theory seems to have no observable consequences whatsoever. Whenever an electron, say, decides to leave us, it is instantly replaced by an identical electron. Since the electrons cannot be told apart, there is no way that we can determine that anything has happened.

What, then, is the point of it all? Is Hawking engaging in a theoretical exercise that has no relevance to anything? Well, not quite. There is a bit more to it than that. According to Hawking, if such a process of particle exchange does take place, this could explain why particles have the particular mass and electric charge that they possess. Passing from one universe to another might be what gives an electron a certain precise mass, and charges it with a unit of electricity.

BUT IS IT SCIENCE?

When one studies certain of Hawking's ideas, it is hard not to feel awed by the profundity of his conceptions. At the same time, one sometimes has the sneaking suspicion that this kind of thing really isn't science any more. For example, the concept of imaginary time may be a brilliant idea. However, if imaginary time ever did exist, this only happened at a point billions of years in the past. We may never be able to find out whether this conception has any relation to reality or not. Hawking has made the idea of a universe without beginning or end plausible. But he has done no more than that. He has only shown that it is possible to conceive of the universe in this manner if one likes.

One part of the imaginary time theory could conceivably be disproved. If we were ever to discover that the universe contains too little mass—and thus insufficient gravitational retarding force—to halt the present expansion, then we will be able to deduce that there can never be a big crunch. The Hawking–Hartle idea of a universe that "ends" in imaginary time will have been shown to be impossible.

On the other hand, the wormhole theory may not be falsifiable at all. It is possible that we will never know whether or not wormholes or other universes really exist. And if we can't know these things, then Hawking's theory becomes something that bears greater resemblance to an artistic creation than it does to a theoretical structure that describes the real world. Hawking's ideas may be beautiful and compelling. But if they lack of empirical character, they are beautiful and compelling only in an aesthetic sense, not in a scientific one.

SCIENCE AS ART OR METAPHYSICS

Stephen Hawking has been confined to a wheelchair for many years. The progressive neurological disease of which he is a victim has now taken away even his powers of speech. One might be tempted to argue *ad hominen* and to suggest that he might have good reasons for wanting to leave the real world behind.

I really think that one should resist the temptation, however. Because Stephen Hawking is not the only scientist who is creating theoretical structures that sometimes seem more like poetry or metaphysics than science. For example, the "hot" theoretical topic in physics right now is that of superstrings. Superstrings are hypothetical ten-dimensional objects of which everything—all known subatomic particles and possibly even space and time—might be made. If superstring theory eventually proves to be correct, a great scientific advance will have been achieved. Superstring theory could very well prove to be a "theory of everything," that is, a theory on which all of the known laws of physics could be based.

However, if superstring theory ever is shown to be correct, this event will surely take place at some point far in the future. Superstring theory is mathematically very difficult, and there is much about it that scientists do not yet understand. The theory has not yet yielded any testable predictions, and most physicists doubt that it will be possible to subject it to experimental test anytime in this century. It isn't even certain what the ten dimensions in which superstrings exist really are. Initially, these were taken to be nine dimensions of space and one dimension of time. But some physicists have suggested that these shouldn't be thought of as space–time dimensions at all, that they are ten not-yet-defined "things."

An enormous quantity of theoretical labor has been expended on superstring theory. So far, there have been few useful results. So naturally this theoretical endeavor has its critics. For example, Nobel Prize–winning physicist Sheldon Glashow and his Harvard University colleague Paul Ginsparg have suggested that the pursuit of superstring theory can be equated to "medieval theology." Faith in an untestable scientific idea, they charge, is replacing science. And the late Richard Feynman, another Nobel laureate, expressed a similar opinion in his typically brash manner. According to Feynman, superstring theories were "nonsense."

Glashow, Ginsparg, and Feynman were clearly perturbed by the fact that so much theoretical energy should be expended on ideas which have, as yet, few connections to the real world. I would argue, however, that this is increasingly the pattern in the more advanced areas of cosmology and physics. Theory has always had a tendency to run ahead of experiment. This tendency can only be exacerbated in our time, when there are so many good theoretical scientists, and when experimental projects become so large and expensive. Experimental technology is limited by certain physical constraints, and there are always funding problems as well. The creative imagination, on the other hand, whether it applies itself to science or to the arts, knows no boundaries.

WHAT NEXT?

When one looks at the scientific work of a Galileo, a Darwin, or an Einstein, one is struck by the emphasis that these scientists placed on creative vision, and by their disregard for conflicting experimental results. But at least it was possible for their theories to be tested.

Today, on the other hand, as theories in physics have become more far-reaching, the scientific imagination has developed a tendency to soar so high that some of the ideas now being proposed may never be confirmed or rejected. Because Stephen Hawking is so brilliant, numerous examples can be found in his work. But he is not the only theoretical scientist who is producing work of this sort. There are numerous other physicists who are engaging in speculation of such a character that it is impossible to tell whether they are trying to describe our universe, or attempting to invent scientifically logical, but wholly imaginary, worlds of their own.

And of course this brings up all manner of questions. Perhaps the most important one is, "What will theoretical physics become?" Will it, as scientists like Glashow and Feynman feared, harden into some new dogma and come to resemble medieval theology? Or will it be more like the metaphysical speculation engaged in by some of the idealist philosophers of the nineteenth century? Or would we be better off thinking of it as some exotic new kind of poetry?

Or will the trend be reversed and theory and experiment make contact with one another again?

Nobody knows.

REVEYESED I'S*

PAT PERRIN

The poet Apollinaire, who wrote newspaper reviews of art exhibits during the years from 1902 to 1918, was an interpreter and supporter of the cubists and other artists of the changing paradigm. He quoted a "bourgeois" as saying to his wife "loud enough for everyone to hear: 'Obviously, the people who like this stuff don't have eyes constructed like ours.' "[1] —

"I LEFT HIM very soon after that," Marie is saying. She speaks with a pronounced French accent which I will not attempt to reproduce here. The thin white-haired woman is sitting with several other people in an art studio classroom. The room is . . . oh, I have been there many times, but it is difficult to recall precisely. The room is nearly square. Several large tables occupy the center of the floor. Tall windows fill one wall. The ceiling is high. Two sinks are set into counters. Tonight, sketches in black and white are pinned up on the walls.

At one side of the room, there is an arrangement, a conglomeration of items—several chairs, some draped fabrics, three colorful gourds, two clay pots, a mannequin dressed as a Gypsy woman, or perhaps it is a human model.

"You left your husband?" asks Karen. She is middle-aged, plain, and practical. But her expression implies that she might have considered the same thing.

"Yes, it was something of a scandal at the time. But then I

---

*The "excerpts from lectures" (passages in italics) are taken from a 1986 dissertation by Pat Perrin, "A Change of Vision: The Emergence of the Systems Paradigm in the Visual, Literary, and Dramatic Arts," or from other papers by the same author.

just didn't care. Later, he divorced me as quietly as he could."

"You left him because of his eyes."

"Because he was right. His eyes weren't constructed to focus on certain things and neither were mine."

A well-groomed man, Roger, looks impatiently at his watch. "The teacher is ten minutes late," he says. He opens a wooden box and begins to lay out tubes of acrylic paints in a neat row on the table. "Do you suppose that we are expected to work from that?" He gestures toward the array of miscellaneous items.

"Probably just from some part of it. I hope," Rose Ellen answers, ducking her head shyly. She also begins to unpack her art materials.

Roger smooths his graying hair with one hand. He takes charcoal in the other hand and begins to sketch on a canvas-covered board.

"You left him because he couldn't stand to look at the cubist work?" Karen persists.

"If that's a problem, I'm afraid that I share it. Not liking cubism, I mean," says Kay, a college student, speaking up for the first time.

The other man in the group stands up restlessly and crosses the room to one of the windows. His name is Paul. Outside, he sees the campus displayed in shades of gray. He looks down on several miniature scenes isolated by the light from lamps on poles, separated by the dark. A couple appears in one of the patches of light, fades into the gray, and reappears under another lamp. The two people seem changed, somehow. Above, the sky is black. "How long do we wait for this teacher to show up?" he asks no one in particular.

Inside, this building is quiet except for a soft medley of distant murmurs. All the other classes have already started. Professors are lecturing, showing slides, demonstrating new techniques. Here, where the evening classes meet, voices are speaking of literature, science, philosophy, various kinds of history. Overlapping words flow out of room after room, down the long hallway, throughout the first and second floors.

In 1923, Virginia Woolf identified a cultural change . . .

Atoms, Niels Bohr reminded his student . . .

Bicycles, radios, telephones, roads, and automobiles . . .

*The poet Apollinaire, who wrote newspaper
reviews . . .*

Only in the studio art class do students chat idly, waiting
for a teacher to appear.

Marie is still talking. "There I was, don't you see?—staring
directly at a completely different vision of the world—things
broken down to their essential geometries, bits of things from
the real world all mixed together. I had absolutely no . . ."
She struggles for the right word. Finally she shrugs and simply
says, "I had no mechanisms for understanding it, none at all."

*In 1923, Virginia Woolf identified a cultural change: "On or about
December, 1910, human character changed. . . . All human relations
have shifted—those between masters and servants, husbands and wives,
parents and children. And when human relations change there is at the
same time a change in religion, conduct, politics, and literature."[2]*

"What did you do after you left your husband?" Karen asks.

Marie smiles. "I lived for some years with an artist, a painter,
there in Paris. I wanted to be around those people who were
seeing things so differently. I wanted to learn how it was
possible that they could conceive of the things they were
painting."

"And did you find out?" asks Rose Ellen.

"Well, I had to revise my eyes," says Marie, with a mis-
chievous grin. I get the impression that she has told this story
before, don't you? "But that accomplished what I wanted to
do, you see, when I left my first husband." She tilts her head
back. In the overhead light her eyes glitter as though they each
have a dozen facets.

"I was so very young when we married. But my father had
been a teacher. I could read and do numbers, although I knew

very little about the sciences. When I watched those young painters at work . . ."

"Did you know them?" a new voice asks breathlessly. "Did you know Picasso and Braque and all those people?" Dark-skinned Olivia is also a college student picking up extra credits at night. She is trying to do the math—could this old lady actually have been alive back then?

"Not very well," Marie answers. She sees that she is losing Karen's interest now and that Paul is gazing at her skeptically. But the two young women, Kay and Olivia, are sitting across the table from her, staring. Marie is flustered. She pulls a handkerchief from her bag and wipes her mouth. She feels, as often happens, somewhat at odds with the wrinkled, veined, and spotted old hands that perform her actions.

Now Marie smiles faintly, in reverie. What is she dreaming of, this woman adrift so far beyond her own time? Is she telling us the truth? She begins to speak again, but gradually her voice grows distant, and then trails off, "During those years, artists of so many kinds began to disregard the time and space that we had known . . . They were trying to bring something quite different into focus . . . sometimes I felt that we all stood on an edge . . . of new definitions . . . of everything . . ."

Atoms, Niels Bohr reminded his student, Heisenberg, were not things—atoms were connections and relationships.

"Do you mean to say that the cubists were basing their work on physics?" asks Paul, walking back from his window. He is a slender man in a turtleneck shirt. No, that's not quite right. He wears something more current—a sweatshirt with some kind of slogan on the front.

Marie looks up with a start. She isn't entirely sure what she has been saying. "On physics? Oh no. I don't think that the artists, the cubists or any of the others, knew anything about physics." Her voice becomes distant again, "It was more like they were . . . asking the same kinds of questions. But it was *in* those paintings and sculptures—the new physics, although we didn't know it then. Things inhabited various kinds of space and different moments of time, seen all at the same time, seeming fragmented, but connected in some different way."

Marie sits up straighter and speaks pertly, "I don't think I ever heard any of them talk about science—painters aren't usually very good explainers, anyhow. But they said, 'that's the way it is.' They believed that."

Heisenberg pointed out fundamental uncertainties about the nature of reality. But he said that we have "not found the correct language with which to speak about the new situation." The difficulty, Heisenberg pointed out, was that "the ordinary language was based on the old concepts of space and time. . . . Yet the experiments showed that the old concepts could not be applied everywhere."[3]

"I'm quite familiar with the notions suggested by quantum physics. At least from a layman's perspective. But how could artists arrive at the same ideas? About reality? Not on their own." Yes, that sounds like Paul. That is just how he talks, in those short, clipped phrases.

"And, no matter what those scientists discovered by their experiments and their mathematics, that's all theory," Kay says firmly. She catches the disapproval on several faces. "What I mean is—it's all microscopic or something like that. It's not the way the world *looks*."

Braque said that he no longer believed in things. "Objects do not exist for me except in so far as a rapport exists between them and between them and myself. In other words, it is not the objects that matter to me but what is in between them."[4]

"Are you saying that art should only deal with the way the world looks?" asks Roger.

"What about self-expression?" asks Olivia.

"What about emotions?" asks Rose Ellen.

"What about dreams and nightmares?" asks Karen.

"Well, I'm talking about visual art and the visual world," says Kay.

"I'm going to check the office. To see if anybody can tell

us anything about this class. I want to know if the teacher is going to show," says Paul. He walks rather stiffly out the door and down the hall. Do you suppose that his casual and contemporary attire may be something of a disguise?

"There is a book out now about art and science. I remember reading something about it. I guess the author says that artists have a special connection to some greater intelligence, so they know what's changing in the world," says Rose Ellen.

Bicycles, radios, telephones, roads, and automobiles—miles of telegraph wires—all made and symbolized connections. People came to realize that more things were happening, all at once, in more places, than they had ever thought about.

"I never thought so," Marie laughs. "They just lived in the world. Things were happening. Maybe they were more sensitive to it." She hesitates and thinks for a moment. "Actually, it wasn't anything that other people didn't know. But at that time, no one could seem to put it into words—the changes we were feeling. It wasn't long before some of the writers did, of course. But the painters could work with the images before they had the words."

"I know there is a powerful inertia in language," says Roger.

"Yes, visual arts can mean new things before we know it," says Marie.

"We're still trying to explain it in words, I guess," says Rose Ellen.

"Lots of people don't like anything they can't explain. And lots of people still don't understand the cubists," says Kay.

"Lots of people haven't given any thought to modern science, either. Except technology," says Roger.

"Technology is what we have," says Karen. "I mean, telephones, automobiles. That's what affects our lives."

"And computer networks," adds Olivia.

"And they still don't like modern art," Kay finishes.

"It's been a hard century to get used to. There's been a lot to absorb," says Marie. She takes off her glasses and rubs her multifaceted eyes.

"Is he well known? Your artist, I mean," asks Rose Ellen. I know I have said very little about this woman. Do you wonder about her age, her appearance? Probably not. Wistful and romantic, Rose Ellen tends to go unnoticed.

"No. He's pretty much forgotten, poor man. He worked very hard at it—at being a genius and all that," says Marie.

"Were you an artist, too?" asks Rose Ellen.

"No, not I. I was not intense enough. And we were still living with the Renaissance tradition of genius, believe me! The members of the avant-garde were quite old-fashioned in that regard," says Marie.

"What do you mean?" asks Olivia, leaning forward intently.

"The Renaissance tradition? Do you mean the discovery of individuality?" asks Kay.

"It was more a definition than a discovery. And some people were thought to be more individual than others," says Marie.

Olivia laughs abruptly. "We still do that. The special ones surrounded by the less special—to whom they accord less reality," she says.

"It's the star system. Kings and geniuses, actors and athletes and CEOs," says Roger.

"And if we're all individuals?" asks Karen.

"That's what got to be a problem. When we say this, that, and the next person is an individual in one way or another—well, if the genius is an individual incapable of maintaining personal relationships with other *individuals,* then the sense of separation becomes acute, painful," says Marie.

"Is that what happened to you?" Karen asks.

"Oh, yes. After we spent several years together, he found that he couldn't get away from me fast enough. He had to find someone less real," Marie answers. For a moment she seems about to wander off into her reveries again. Then she says firmly, "Dichotomies. We still have a problem with them."

A voice from the other side of the room startles the entire group, "Science/superstition; objective/subjective; intelligence/emotions; rational/irrational; conscious/unconscious; object/symbol; reality/art."

Their heads all jerk around. The model steps down from the composition of subjects. "Self and not-self, the viewer and the viewed, participant and observer," she intones mournfully.

Kay and Rose Ellen both look as though they might get up and run. But at that moment, Paul returns.

"The office is locked up. All the other classes are in session. I don't even know who to call at this time of night. I guess this class is a bust," says Paul.

He begins to gather his belongings together, but the rest of the group ignores him. The model has taken a seat at the table, opposite Marie. Finally, Paul comes and sits down at the table, too.

"That's right. And genius/not-genius, creative/non-creative, individual/non-person. It's an attitude problem they all had. In the end, they suffered terribly from it," says Marie.

"Don't great artists always suffer? Don't they truly have a superior gift of some kind? Doesn't he—or she—reach things the rest of us can't? Don't ideas break through suddenly in creative explosions, and carry the genius into whole new universes?" asks Rose Ellen.

Poincaré described his experience of working repeatedly on a problem without results: "I was then very ignorant; every day I seated myself at my work table, stayed an hour or two, tried a great number of combinations and reached no results. One evening, contrary to my custom, I drank black coffee and could not sleep. Ideas rose in crowds; I felt them collide until pairs interlocked . . ."[5]

"That's our definition. Do you think it's final—an absolute of some kind? I mean, maybe that explosion of ideas happens because the flow of ideas has habitually been blocked. Maybe there's another way to do it," says the model in the Gypsy dress.

"Or a lot of other ways," says Olivia, thoughtfully.

"But Marie, if the artists were working on things the rest of us still have trouble seeing—doesn't that mean they were somehow different?" Rose Ellen persists.

"Well, they were eager to look. That's something. They clung ferociously to their avenues of creative insight. They took terrible risks. They were willing to throw themselves into conflict with their culture," Marie answers, tentatively.

"There is a limit, I suppose, to the degree of revision any of us can do on our perceptions—all at once," says the model, looking inquiringly at Marie.

"Oh, I don't blame them. I'm sorry for the pain it caused them. After all, it's a cultural definition of creativity that has not changed so very much since then," says Marie.

"Because we have not been able to imagine other possibilities? Are there other possibilities?" asks Rose Ellen.

"How can we tell? Anything that doesn't meet our definition of a creative act might go unnoticed," says the model.

"Maybe that's why there have never seemed to be many really creative women. Because we don't like to hold it all back until it breaks out suddenly," says Karen.

"And if we change our definitions?" asks Roger.

"Definitions change," says Marie, shrugging.

In 1909, John Dewey wrote: "The conceptions that had reigned in the philosophy of nature and knowledge for two thousand years, the conceptions that had become the familiar furniture of the mind, rested on the assumption of the superiority of the fixed and final; they rested upon treating change and origin as signs of defect and unreality."[6]

The model laughs. Scornfully, she says, "In one period, religion gave our culture an image of reality within which to live. In a later time, mind defined the universe, or promised to, and then science showed us how the answers could be found. In our time, without any scheme for determining final answers, we revert to defining our terms."

"What are you talking about? Do you think that all those definitions were wrong?" asks Kay.

"Not wrong. Insufficient. Not absolute, as they would have had us think. And we always try to turn a definition into a dichotomy—making everything that or not-that—noticing nothing in between."

Light behaves like a wave and like a particle, Bohr said. Both views are necessary—that's just the way it is.

"If you redesign your eyes enough times, absolutes are hard to come by. The cubists pulled back to include both versions of some things in the same view," says Marie.

"What you're talking about can make a culture, or a life, very unstable, very complicated," says Roger.

"Maybe it would be less of a problem if we just didn't insist on defining everything," says the model.

"How Zen you sound," says Paul. That doesn't sound exactly like a compliment. But Olivia nods and agrees.

"Traditionally, the Japanese believe that words and explanations are, themselves, detrimental to understanding. They use illustrations, stories and sayings, and they teach skills. But not definitions or directions," says Olivia.

"A conception is not a reality. And words are likely to lead one away from the *experience* of reality . . . and into the unreality of a conception," says the model.

"Their art was more a way of achieving a certain state of mind. Or, an indication that it has been achieved," says Olivia.

"Traditionally, we pursued skills and a state of mind in order to accomplish art, while the Japanese pursued skills and art in order to achieve a state of mind," says the model.

When Eugen Herrigel had worked persistently over a period of years, but was still not able to grasp the frame of mind necessary to a master archer, his teacher made an effort to find other ways to communicate the ideas to him. Since Herrigel was teaching philosophy at the University of Tokyo, the master archer had "tried to work through a Japanese introduction to philosophy in order to find out how he could help me from a side I already knew. But in the end he had laid the book down with a cross face, remarking that he could now understand that a person who interested himself in such things would naturally find the art of archery uncommonly difficult to learn."[7]

"And the Japanese tradition didn't include the same concept of the superior individual, of the separated genius," says Olivia.

Roger grimaces and says, "Maybe that's why their CEOs only make twenty times what their line workers do. So, I guess that's it! A Renaissance hangover led us to glorify our CEOs and reward them with a hundred times the pay of our workers."

A sudden babble of voices in the hallway announces that some of the other evening classes are taking a break.

"I'm going to see what I can find out," says Paul.

"I'm going to get a drink of water," says Kay. She and Olivia wander out of the room. Roger and Rose Ellen strike up a conversation and go out, too. As they leave, we can hear him saying, "I needed some kind of hobby, something to help me relax."

The model wanders around the room, rearranging things. Looking at the sketches on the wall, she reaches out and puts her hand on a red brush stroke that defines a human form. Then she touches a blue slash that indicates a table. She nods. She goes to the group of objects at the side of the room and begins adding new items.

Karen moves over where she can sit closer to Marie.

"What did you do, then? When your artist friend left you," she asks.

"Oh, I became a governess. The people were gallery patrons and they were happy to take me on. Later I married a young physicist, and began to find out all the incredible things that scientists were looking into. Eventually, we moved to this country. It has been an exciting time," Marie answers.

"My goodness, from artists to scientists."

"It wasn't such a big change."

"It can't be the same in art and science. One has to do with reality. The other is just imagination. Scientists are working with real data, with facts," says Karen.

"Facts, yes. That's not what was exciting," says Marie.

"A lot of facts are trivial," the model says, considering a vase that she holds in her hands. Is it ceramic or plastic? Shall we test it? Shall we count the numbers of each we find within the room?

Kay and Olivia have just reentered the classroom. Kay

laughs. "You mean all those statistics I've been gathering won't do any good?"

The model sighs deeply. "We've sure bought that whole story—in the humanities. We got on the reality bandwagon. We started measuring everything in sight."

"What?" asks Kay.

"Before long, we were only thinking about things we could measure." She sighs deeply. "The whole scramble for justification through explanation, validation through data, recognition through whole vocabularies—code-words, in-words. Focus on analyzable processes, evading everything else."

Kay sits down and stares at the model. "The scientist's measurements are important," she says.

"Important, of course. But not always interesting," says Marie.

"Technology is exciting and essential," says Kay.

"Yes, in its pragmatic way. But creative science is just as blind and risky as creative art. In our culture, it's been a case of appreciating scientists for the wrong reasons," the model replies.

"The best of the scientists may work from an empirical base, but they also come back with new questions, find out things they weren't looking for, consider implications—they *philosophize*," says Olivia.

"Exactly. While philosophers and art educators and literary theorists have decided to measure and explain. And stick to what they *can* measure and explain. And accept those artists who know the terms, who fit the explanations," says Marie.

"Just defining our terms, defining our terms," says the model.

Paul comes back into the room. "I can't find out anything about this class. I'm going home." He gathers up his belongings and, this time, he leaves. He goes out of the building into the night, moving through the patches of light and dark, unchanged.

Roger and Rose Ellen also come back into the room and begin packing up their art supplies.

Karen leans over and asks Marie, "Why are you taking an art class now?"

"I became a poet," says Marie. "I had a wonderful time searching with the words. My husband and I talked about everything. But he is gone now and I'm still here."

"I don't understand."

"There are things I sense that I can't put into words. Maybe it's just that I can't redo my eyes anymore. That's all right, if that's the way it's going to be. But I thought that, maybe, the shapes and colors might lead me somewhere."

Just as Roger and Rose Ellen are leaving together, Roger turns back and looks at Marie. "Why did they persist? Why do you?" he asks.

"What?" asks Marie.

"Why do artists insist on making art, without pay or recognition?" Roger asks.

"Why is art made, when the artist is no longer employed to fill the needs of church or king? Why, when there are no animals to be entranced, no hunting spells to weave by firelight deep beneath the earth? When images can more quickly be made by other means?" the model chants.

"When there is no clear *use* for what they do?" Roger asks.

"The artist needs to get the intuitions of the mind outside, and see what they look like. Or hear what they sound like," Marie answers.

"Thoughts grow and change as they emerge. The process of getting the images down is a process of knowing them better. It's a way of coming to terms with the shifting and expanding nature of reality," the model says.

"What does creativity have to do with reality?" Kay asks.

"I think that the relationship of art to reality lies in the creative act itself. It's not in the images or other results produced. The creation of images is part of the learning process, not something carried out after it," says Marie.

"Just for themselves, then?" asks Roger.

"Oh, no. The response of others adds to the meaning. When readers and viewers make their own meanings, they are also involved in the process," says Marie.

162 PAT PERRIN

Sergei Eisenstein felt that a synthesis could be reached by the viewer. Meaning grows from the relationship of ideas. "It is precisely the montage principle, as distinguished from that of representation, which obliges spectators themselves to create, and the montage principle, by this means, achieves that great power of inner creative excitement in the spectator which distinguishes an emotionally exciting work from one that stops going further than giving information or recording events."[8]

"But what does all of that have to do with living in the real world?" Kay asks.

"It is by focusing on the process of creating works of art, and by drawing the viewer into that process, that our arts represent the real world. They reflect the way that we function in that world," says the model. She returns to her place among the still-life items.

The model sits still for a long moment, then shifts her position. She speaks slowly, " 'No longer to receive ready-made a world completed, full, closed upon itself, but on the contrary to participate in a creation, to invent in his turn the work—and the world—and thus to learn to invent his own life.' "[9] She says nothing more. But that last, I am sure, was a quote from Robbe-Grillet. I shall have to look it up.

Marie nods. She gets slowly to her feet and gathers up her belongings. "My grandson is coming for me after class. But that's still a long time off."

"I'll give you a ride home," says Karen.

"Are there artists now, discovering?" asks Olivia.

"I hope so. I trust there must be," says Marie. Once more, we glimpse through her glasses the multiple lights reflecting off her eyes.

Karen and Marie go out together. Kay and Olivia remain for a short time, talking quietly. Am I mistaken, or do I see there a slight glitter, a hint of a change in the eyes?

Then they, too, go out into the dark.

As artists of all kinds have discovered, Woolf says that it is by working in the medium that the idea is completed: "From this I reach what I might call a philosophy; at any rate it is a constant idea of mine; that

behind the cotton wool is hidden a pattern; that we—I mean all human
beings—are connected with this; that the whole world is a work of art;
that we are parts of the work of art. . . ."[10]

NOTES

1. Guillaume Apollinaire, *Apollinaire on Art: Essays and Reviews 1902–1918*, translated by Leroy C. Breunig, edited by Susan Suleiman (New York: The Viking Press, 1972), p. 462.

2. Virginia Woolf, in *The Virginia Woolf Reader,* edited by Mitchell A. Leaska (San Diego: Harcourt Brace Jovanovich, 1985), pp. 194–195.

3. Werner Heisenberg, *Physics and Philosophy: The Revolution in Modern Science* (New York: Harper & Row, 1958), pp. 167 and 174.

4. Translation by John Richardson in his *G. Braque* (Greenwich, CT: New York Graphic Society, 1961), pp. 23–24.

5. Henri Poincaré, "Mathematical Creation," in Brewster Ghiselin, *The Creative Process* (New York: New American Library, 1952), p. 36.

6. John Dewey, *The Influence of Darwinism on Philosophy* (Bloomington: Indiana University Press, 1965), p. 1.

7. Eugen Herrigel, *Zen in the Art of Archery* (New York: Pantheon Books, 1953), p. 24.

8. Sergei Eisenstein, *The Film Sense,* edited and translated by Jay Leyda (New York: Meridian, 1957), p. 35.

9. Alain Robbe-Grillet, *For a New Novel* (New York: Grove Press, Inc., 1965), p. 156.

10. Virginia Woolf, "A Sketch of the Past," in *The Virginia Woolf Reader,* p. 11.

THE CREATIVE BRAIN

RICHARD RESTAK, M.D.

ASK THE QUESTION "What are the five personal qualities you most desire for yourself?" and the response, "creativity . . . the ability to be creative," is almost as certain to turn up on the list as health, good looks, charm, and sexual prowess. One of the reasons many people wish to be creative is their recognition that creativity can help them attain almost any other goal they set for themselves.

Attempts at understanding and nourishing creativity traditionally concentrate on social, psychological, and cultural contributions. Unfortunately this bypasses the ultimate determinant of creativity: the human brain. Recent research reveals that various aspects of creativity are mediated and nourished by specific organizational patterns within the brain. This is not the same thing as saying that creativity can be explained on a strictly neurologic basis—a form of reductionism Arthur Koestler rightly criticized as "nothing buttery"—but it does suggest that some understanding of the brain may contribute toward that desire for personal creativity.

When the two brain hemispheres are compared, the right seems particularly important in the visual and performing arts. Numerous studies on normals, neurosurgical patients, and brain-injured people reveal that the right hemisphere is generally dominant for recognizing and identifying natural and nonverbal sounds. It is better at appreciating depth perception; maintaining a sense of body image; producing dreams during REM sleep; and appreciating and expressing the emotion aroused by

164

music and the visual arts. Finally, the right hemisphere is specialized for perceiving emotional expression in others and generating it in oneself.

Damage to the right hemisphere results in distortions in the appreciation of music and natural sounds. In addition a host of neuropsychiatric expressions—all of them germane to creativity—may arise. These include indifference and loss of "drive," depression, manic excitement, euphoria, impulsivity, delusions, and perceptual distortions in regard to the body.

"The right hemisphere maintains a highly developed social-emotional mental system and can independently perceive, recall and act on certain memories and experiences without the aid or active reflective participation of the left hemisphere,"[1] according to R. Joseph of the Neurobehavioral Center in Santa Clara, California.

Joseph is describing on the neurological level what every creative person experiences regularly—creative ideas and images seeming to spring "out of the blue" which might more accurately be characterized as out of the right hemisphere. "Of the truly creative no one is ever master; it must be left to go its own way," as Goethe described the serendipitous ways of creativity.

In all instances personal insight into the source of one's creativity is hampered by the fact that:

> We know more than we can say: we live
> in waves and feelings of awareness
> where images unfold and grow
> along the leafwork of our nerves and
> veins . . .

as poet Peter Meinke describes the process in his poem "Azaleas."

With writers and other creative individuals who work with words, the right-hemisphere contribution is undoubtedly much different. Since language and verbal centers are in the left hemisphere, writers are capable, at least in theory, of continuing to be creative in the face of right-brain damage. What usually stops them is one or more of the emotional sequelae of right-brain damage mentioned above.

Split-brain patients provide an unusual opportunity to explore the mutual interactions between brain organization and creativity. These patients—referred to as "split brain" because of a surgically created separation of the right and left hemispheres—behave perfectly normally in ordinary social situations. Despite their apparent normality they show little creativity as measured by tests of language, thinking, and emotional expression. They lack the ability to transform the imagery and symbols generated by the right hemisphere into creative verbalizations.

Dr. Klaus D. Hoppe, a psychiatrist at the Hacker Clinic in Los Angeles, believes that the absence of creativity in split-brain patients is similar to what is observed in people suffering from alexithymia,[2] a term taken from the Greek meaning "without words for feelings." People with alexithymia have great difficulty in identifying and verbalizing their feelings. And although the term is rarely encountered, alexithymics are far from rare. They appear frequently in medical clinics and doctors' offices. Typically they experience and express emotional stress by developing physical symptoms. Insight into the psychological origin of their distress eludes them. Moreover, they vigorously deny inner feelings and seem to inhabit a robotic inner life devoid of the finer shades of emotional experience. As a result they are oblivious to suggestions that "stress" or other emotional factors may be playing a role in their illness. Needless to say, alexithymics are difficult and frustrating patients to care for.

Creativity is the opposite of alexithymia. As a rule, creative individuals are "in touch" with their feelings and express them through their creative productions. At the neurological level this involves an enriched communication between the hemispheres—bisociation—rather than the hemisphere dissociation typical of the split-brain patient. The more creative one is, the more likely the two sides of the brain are in easy communication with each other. In support of this are EEG studies carried out by Hoppe and associates: they found greater coherence and interhemispheric communication between the two hemispheres in creative people.[3]

"It is now certain that the corpus callosum can transfer high-level information from one hemisphere to another,"[4] according to UCLA neurosurgeon Joseph E. Bogen, who carried out early research on split-brain operations in humans. Bogen suggests that the neurological underpinnings of creativity may require not only good communication between the hemispheres but "a partial (and transiently reversible) hemispheric independence" whereby one hemisphere may for a time independently engage in creative production outside of immediate conscious awareness. This could explain the "aha!" response: "the illumination that precedes subsequent deliberate verification." Anticipating such developments years ago, neuroscientist Frederick Bremer wrote that the corpus callosum, by uniting the activities of the two hemispheres, makes possible "the highest and most elaborate activities of the brain"—and what can fit this description better than creativity?

A good model of the creative process is suggested by Albert Rothenberg, clinical professor of psychiatry at Harvard Medical School. He speaks of homospatial thinking: "actively conceiving two or more discrete entities occupying the same space."[5] In order to test this hypothesis, Rothenberg showed forty-three artists three sets of slide photographs (each set consisted of two different slides—for example, five racehorses rounding the turn paired with a separate slide of five nuns walking together in Vatican Square). Some of the artists were shown the slides aligned side by side on the projection screen while others viewed the slides superimposed on each other. Each artist was then asked to create a pastel drawing stimulated by each of the three slide pairs. Two internationally prominent artists evaluated the drawings. They judged drawings stimulated by the superimposed slides as significantly more creative than drawings resulting from the separated slides.

Nor is homospatial thinking limited to drawing and the visual arts. Rothenberg believes creative people in literature, music, science, and mathematics excel in their ability to intermingle and superimpose elements from many different spatial and temporal dimensions. He calls this *janusian* thinking: actively conceiving two or more opposites or antitheses simultaneously during the course of the creative process. These internal conceptions can be opposite or antithetical words, ideas, or images. After clarification and definition, they are either conceptualized side by side and/or as coexisting simultaneously. Finally they are modified, transformed, or otherwise employed in creative productions in the arts, sciences, or other fields.

In a test of janusian thinking Rothenberg administered timed word association tests to 12 creative Nobel laureates, 18 hospitalized patients, and 113 college students divided into categories of high and low creativity. The Nobel laureates gave the highest proportion of opposite (unusual) responses. They also furnished these opposite responses at significantly faster rates than common responses. Indeed, their average speed of opposite response was fast enough to indicate that conceptualizing the opposites could have been simultaneous. Rothenberg thinks of these highly creative people as engaging in a "translogical process."

Homospatial thinking and janusian thinking correspond in neurological terms to the actions of the frontal and prefrontal lobes. Thanks to these brain areas, which are more evolved in the human brain than in the brain of any other creature, we can mentally access information and keep it on-line (that is, in mind) until it is integrated into one's ongoing plans. Thanks to this ability to bind time we are able to hold on-line real or imaginal ideas that form the basis for creativity. We can internally rehearse and anticipate the consequences of our actions, and introduce innovative and novel responses. We know this because, after frontal and prefrontal damage, the injured person is reduced to living in a here-and-now world in which future consequences and possibilities exert little influence on present behavior and preoccupations. Such persons have great difficulty managing new situations or demands and almost never initiate innovative activities on their own. In a phrase, the victim of frontal-lobe damage is at the opposite end of the spectrum from the creative person.

A high degree of cortical arousal (heightened responsiveness to the events and people in one's environment) is also a prerequisite for creativity. Since introverts characteristically show high cortical arousal, it's not surprising that, in general, creativity comes easier to introverts and those with emotionally responsive dispositions. "Creativity is a problem-solving response by intelligent, very active, highly emotional, and extremely introverted persons,"[6] according to Dr. L. M. Bachtold, who over the past decade has concentrated on understanding the neurophysiological basis of creativity. His findings suggest to me that if there is a neurological basis for creativity, a single distinguishing trait separating the creative from others, it will be discovered within the frontal and prefrontal areas.

"Subjected to a vast array of disorganized perceptual data and strongly feeling the inconsistencies, the active and intelligent individual forms new perceptual relationships to develop feelings of consistency and harmony," says Bachtold.

But there is a hazard in deriving one's neurological concepts about creativity strictly on the basis of observing the effects of deficits resulting from brain damage. It's always possible that the injured brain area may be only a small contributor to creativity, important enough to stymie the creative process but not at all its major impetus. Furthermore, there are rare instances on record where brain damage *enhanced* creativity.

An artisan in his mid-twenties began to experience attacks marked by the feeling he was floating helplessly in space. During these episodes in which "waves" engulfed him he would begin drawing impulsively. This behavior was all the more remarkable since he had never previously expressed any interest in drawing or artistic activity.

An EEG showed epileptic seizure discharges within the frontal and temporal lobes on the left. Additional tests measuring brain activity levels yielded more evidence of dysfunction in the anterior regions of the left hemisphere.

Although a certain amount of speculation is always involved in explaining strange phenomena like this, and, further, equally qualified observers may hold in good faith different opinions about what's going on, I tend to agree with the opinion of the neurologists who cared for the patient. They speculated that the impulses toward artistic expression resulted from the release, as a result of damage to the left hemisphere, of the complex visual and spatial skills of the right hemisphere. It's as if blockage of this man's customary expressive powers brought on by left-hemisphere injury led to an unusual and unpredictable form of artistic expression.

But despite the fascination engendered by this patient, it's necessary to remind oneself that this artisan is unique, the only example so far of enhanced artistic creation resulting from brain damage. Evey other example I have personally encountered or read about in case reports confirms that brain damage produces a failing, and usually a serious failing, in creative expression.

For example, brain injury to either hemisphere interferes with drawing ability in specific ways. If the right hemisphere is damaged, the drawings lack features on the left side of the picture. This is because right-brain damage results in neglect of persons and objects in the left visual field, which is mediated by the right hemisphere. Spatial relationships are also distorted. Left-brain damage, in contrast, results in overly simplified childlike productions marked by conceptual rather than spatial errors (a drawing of a table setting for one may show three forks).

Probably the most feared form of brain damage results from Alzheimer's disease. And although the cause of this devastating degenerative brain disorder has so far eluded the efforts of neuroscientists around the world, a good bit is known about its effects on creativity.

An elderly artist underwent, over a two-year period, a dramatic deterioration in painting skills and intellectual ability. His artistic skills deteriorated slower than his other mental functions. In fact, until late in his illness, his artistic talents suffered only because of falloffs in motivation, memory, and organizational skills. In normal aging such deteriorations fail to occur.

A study of seventy-year-olds carried out at the University of Gothenburg in 1989 showed that creativity did not decline over a thirteen-year follow-up period. The study was obviously an unusual one since it involved tracking, over more than a decade, individuals already at an advanced age. The measures of creativity were also somewhat unusual: the interpretation of inkblots coded for three components of creativity—fluency, flexibility, and originality.

Rather than declining with age, it's likely that creativity in the older person changes in nature according to the special circumstances of aging. For instance, self-expression for its own sake or as a sublimation for sexual or aggressive urges plays a smaller role. Like it or not, most of us really do mellow with age; even the most ambitious eventually share to some degree that ancient wisdom that recognizes, even in the face of fame and creative accomplishment, the transitoriness of all things. In addition, stylistic and thematic concerns are likely to change in the older creative artist in response to interests different from his younger counterpart. Picasso is an excellent example of the creative artist who retains an ever-evolving creative sense despite the ravages of time and aging.

Creative persons of different ages may also differ in the ways they go about artificially boosting their creativity. For centuries some creative people have relied on chemical aids to spur their creativity. These chemicals include perfectly legal substances like tea (Balzac drank quarts of it during marathon writing sessions), alcohol (Faulkner and Kerouac drank heavily while in the process of composition), and nicotine (innumerable writers have attested to nicotine's power to enhance concentration and focus); also included are other chemicals that are either illegal or available only by prescription (amphetamine, cocaine, or LSD). The real question is, of course, do these chemical aids really stimulate creativity, or are the users only fooling themselves?

In 1989 psychiatrists from the University of California, Irvine, reported on a unique experiment carried out thirty years earlier on the effects of LSD on creativity.[7] Artists were asked to draw and paint a kachina doll. They then took LSD and drew a second doll. When they were finished, a professor of art history analyzed and compared the two productions.

The most significant changes occurred in the works of those artists with representational or abstract styles. Under LSD the paintings were more expressionistic or nonobjective. In almost all cases the artists saw this as "fashioning new meanings to an emergent world." Indicators of this change included relative size expansion, movement, alteration of boundaries and figure/ ground relations, greater intensity of color and light, oversimplification, fragmentation, disorganization, and the symbolic and abstract rendering of people and objects. In short, there seems little reason to doubt that the creative product was different, but was it better?

Of course, this perfectly reasonable question is difficult to answer because of the highly subjective nature of art appreciation. Evaluating whether or not an artist is more creative as a result of taking LSD or another drug is not as easily done as deciding whether a scientist is more creative under the influence of psychoactive chemicals. With the scientist one can perform experiments or check such variables as the number of papers written and the frequency of their citation by other scientists. But what type of measure does one employ for evaluating whether an LSD-influenced work is better than the artist's usual production? One thing is certain: no artist that I am aware of has created under the powers of LSD an acclaimed body of work over an extended period of time. Moreover, I can't help wondering if the artist's claims for the creativity-stimulating effects of LSD are not a variation of what we refer to in medicine as the placebo effect, where such psychological factors as expectations and hopes play an inordinately important role.

When it comes to psychological factors, the creative person must possess what psychologists refer to as ego autonomy. And various neurologic and psychiatric illnesses can impair this sense of autonomy. Obsessions and compulsions interfere with spontaneity and the flexibility that is a requirement for creative breakthroughs. Frontal-lobe disease, as mentioned a moment ago, disrupts programming, novel associations, and persistence. And whatever disease or malfunction interferes with smooth communication from one hemisphere to another prevents the integration and expression that form the basis of all creativity.

But not all emotional and neurological illnesses are incompatible with creativity. Writers have a high prevalence of depression and bipolar disorder (manic-depression). Since alcohol is the most commonly employed self-prescribed medication for depression, it comes as no surprise that alcoholism is also common among writers given to depression. It will be interesting to see if this pattern of alcohol abuse among creative writers will change in response to the current emphasis on health and the mild but definite social stigma attached to alcohol use. Also playing a factor in determining this will be the increasing acceptance of mood disorders as illnesses rather than character flaws, and the associated willingness of writers, artists, and other creative persons to seek help. As things now stand, some creative people refuse treatments such as lithium for bipolar disorder; they claim the medication blunts their sensibilities and lessens their creative powers.

Associations between neuropsychiatric illness and creativity have prompted some psychiatrists to conclude that a touch of madness may enhance creativity. While this is possible in the individual instance, most studies conclude that, in general, creative individuals are most productive when their moods, thoughts, and behavior are under control. Certainly untreated mental illness or brain disease can be expected to interfere with one quality for creativity identified by former world chess champion Max Euwe: "the ability to distinguish with certainty that infinitesimal dividing line between the inspired and the unsound."

Rather than correlating with brain and emotional disorders, creativity seems to be linked with what Freud referred to as ordinary human unhappiness. "We enjoy lovely music, beautiful paintings, a thousand intellectual delicacies, but we have no idea of their cost, to those who invented them, in sleepless nights, tears, spasmodic laughter, rashes, asthmas, epilepsies, and the fear of death, which is worse than all the rest," is how Marcel Proust described the psychological demands made on the creative individual.

One final point about writers. When thirty writers were administered psychological tests, they scored with above-average IQs but failed to do any better than matched controls in any subtest other than vocabulary. This finding is further confirmation of the everyday observation that intelligence and creativity are independent mental abilities. It's possible to be creative although not exceptionally intelligent; the majority of highly intelligent people are not conspicuously creative.

Future research on creativity is likely to dispel another common assertion: that creativity is more likely to be found in the arts rather than the sciences. Such distinctions are illogical and wrongheaded. A mathematical formula can be as creative as a sonnet. And the application of medical knowledge and skill in the service of arriving at a life-saving diagnosis of a serious but treatable illness is the most marvelous creative expression of all: the rescue of life, from which all creativity emerges, from the implacable clutches of death and oblivion. In my own professional life—divided between writing and the practice of neuropsychiatry—I have experienced in these two very different disciplines the joys attendant on creative expression.

No. Creativity doesn't play favorites: it espouses the arts no more or less than the sciences. Thus it's likely that future knowledge about the brain will shed light on the creativity of both the physicist and the dancer, the chemist and the playwright. And why should we expect it to be otherwise, given that the human brain is the progenitor of all creativity?

Arthur Koestler: "Einstein's space is no closer to reality than

Van Gogh's sky. The glory of science is not in a truth more absolute than the truth of Bach or Tolstoy, but in the act of creation itself. The scientist's discoveries impose his own order on chaos, as the composer or painter imposes his—an order that always refers to limited aspects of reality, and is biased by the observer's frame of reference, which differs from period to period, as a Rembrandt nude differs from a nude by Manet."

NOTES

1. R. Joseph, "The Right Cerebral Hemisphere: Emotion, Music, Visual-Spatial Skills, Body-Image, Dreams, and Awareness," *Journal of Clinical Psychology,* 44 (1988): 630–673.
2. K. D. Hoppe, "Hemispheric Specialization and Creativity," *Psychiatric Clinics of North America,* 11 (1988): 303–315.
3. Ibid.
4. J. E. Bogen and G. M. Bogen, "Creativity and the Corpus Callosum," *Psychiatric Clinics of North America,* 11 (1988): 293–301.
5. A. Rothenberg and R. S. Sobel, "Adaptation and Cognition. II. Experimental Study of the Homospatial Process in Artistic Creativity," *Journal of Nervous & Mental Disease,* 169 (1981): 417–423.
6. L. M. Bachtold, "Speculation on a Theory of Creativity: A Physiological Basis," *Perceptual & Motor Skills,* 50 (1980): 699–702.
7. O. Janiger and M. Dobkin de Rios, "LSD and Creativity," *Journal of Psychoactive Drugs,* 21 (1989): 129–134.

GENIUS AND CHANCE: A DARWINIAN PERSPECTIVE

DEAN KEITH SIMONTON

CHARLES DARWIN WAS certainly one of the most influential thinkers of the nineteenth century. He pushed the scientific revolution one vital step further. Copernicus had already displaced the earth as the center of the cosmos. Galileo and Newton had replaced the commonsense physics of Aristotle with a science more mechanical and mathematical. Lavoisier had hammered the final nail on alchemy's coffin. The edge of objectivity had thus cut its way through the physical sciences. It was time to slice away all the medieval residues that remained in the biological sciences.

As the received tradition had it, all species were created by God more or less as described by the book of Genesis. The species were permanent kinds. To be sure, catastrophes could drive some plants or animals to extinction; not everyone was invited aboard Noah's ark. Even so, the principal imprint on the variety of living things was a permanence that only an omniscient and omnipotent Being could establish. Moreover, all of Nature revealed a grand plan. There was purpose, a divine order that guided each creature on this planet. The human species was part of a Great Chain of Being, placed at the fulcrum between the brutes below and the angels above.

Darwin's 1859 *Origin of Species* did away with all this mystical paraphernalia. Life was constantly changing. Old forms

176

were going extinct, new forms emerging. Yet behind all these transformations dwelt no celestial order. Members of a given species exhibited variations in morphological, physiological, and behavioral traits. Some of these variants were more adaptive than others, enabling some individuals to produce more offspring than others. Natural selection superseded the holy design. Not only did species change, but there was no teleology besides. No Superior Being directed the course of evolution. Nor did Darwin endorse the Lamarckian notion of a more limited purpose operating at the individual level. Variations within a species evinced no wisdom, foresight, or volition. And even if natural selection could supply a cornucopia of species well adapted to an ecological niche, we could no longer identify *Homo sapiens* as the acme of the progression.

Needless to say, Darwin's theory was not without flaws. Neo-Darwinism of the twentieth century had to bring it in line with more modern developments, such as Mendelian genetics. Furthermore, even today several tenets of Darwinian thought provoke scientific controversy. The details of biological evolution are far from settled. Nevertheless, none of this debate concerns us here. Instead, I wish to discuss a spinoff of Darwin's revolutionary hypothesis. Darwinian ideas have inspired the framework for a comprehensive theory of creativity.[1] Like Darwin's system, this theory explains the phenomenon without resorting to some *deus ex machina*. This perspective, in fact, destroys many recurring myths about the creative genius.

Below I outline this theory under four headings: (1) thoughts and processes, (2) products and ideas, (3) persons and personalities, and (4) schools and cultures. As we'll see, these headings demarcate the four levels at which Darwinian creativity functions.

THOUGHTS AND PROCESSES

Donald Campbell, the eminent American psychologist, put forward a Darwinian theory of creativity back in 1960. He called it the "blind-variation and selective-retention" model.[2] According to Campbell, creativity entails two essential operations.

First, *variations* must be produced. These variations are re-combinations of the contents of the human brain. The contents can include concepts and percepts, schema, feelings, memories, and anything else that can be subjected to free permutation. A crucial ingredient of this variation process, however, must be its "blindness." Blind variations issue from a basically trial-and-error process—just like the genetic recombinations and mutations in biological evolution. Whether one variation or another appears is due not to some insight or foresight, but rather to happenstance. We will have a lot more to say about this shortly.

Second, these haphazard variations are subjected to a consistent *selection* procedure. This process weeds out all those combinations that lack adaptive fitness in some psychological sense. In other words, there must exist within the creator's mind some stable criteria by which to winnow out the true, beautiful, or useful variations from those that are false, ugly, or impractical. Once selected, the variations must be preserved and reproduced by some *retention* process. In biological evolution, genes that increase adaptive fitness are retained on the chromosomes. In creativity, ideational variations are preserved in memory. Retention can occur at higher levels still.

The foregoing description, while schematic, at least corresponds to the introspective reports of many eminent creators. John Dryden, in his *Dedication of the Rival-Ladies*, noted how his play began "when it was only a confused mass of thoughts, tumbling over one another in the dark; when the fancy was yet in its first work, moving the sleeping images of things towards the light, there to be distinguished, and then either chosen or rejected by the judgment."[3] The French poet and essayist Paul Valéry offered a succinct paraphrase: "It takes two to invent something. The one makes up combinations; the other chooses, recognizes what he wishes and what is important to him in the mass of the things which the former has imparted to him."[4]

Of the two steps, the first is the more interesting. To generate genuinely blind variations requires a special sort of mind. Over a century ago, William James offered an excellent description of the thinking patterns of the creative genius:

> Instead of thoughts of concrete things patiently following one another in a beaten track of habitual suggestion, we have the most abrupt cross-cuts and transitions from one idea to another, the most rarefied abstractions and discriminations, the most unheard of combinations of elements, the subtlest associations of analogy; in a word, we seem suddenly introduced into a seething caldron of ideas, where everything is fizzling and bobbling about in a state of bewildering activity, where partnerships can be joined or loosened in an instant, treadmill routine is unknown, and the unexpected seems only law.[5]

Often this rich associative play occurs via vivid imagery—visual, auditory, even kinesthetic. Other times the mental elements may be connected through such weak associations that the whole variation process dips below the threshold of core consciousness. The French mathematician Jacques Hadamard, after noting the necessity of constructing many combinations, added, "It cannot be avoided that this first operation take place, to a certain extent, at random, so that the role of chance is hardly doubtful in the first step of the mental process. But we see that the intervention of chance occurs inside the unconscious: for most of these combinations—more exactly, all those which are useless—remain unknown to us."[6]

Once a fruitful idea is chanced upon, thought processes become more pedestrian. In psychoanalytic terms, the creator shifts from primary process (Dryden's "fancy") to secondary process (Dryden's "judgment"). Fantastic, unpredictable combinatory play gives way to more rational and deliberate encoding in a more durable, symbolic form. As Albert Einstein expressed it, "conventional words or other signs have to be

sought for laboriously only in a secondary stage, when the
mentioned associative play is sufficiently established and can
be reproduced at will."[7] We must underline the adverb *laboriously*. Because the mental processes by which new ideas
emerge so often bypass verbal representations, it can take con-
siderable effort to translate them into a communicable format.
For instance, Francis Galton once complained:

> It is a serious drawback to me in writing, and still more in
> explaining myself, that I do not so easily think in words as
> otherwise. It often happens that after being hard at work, and
> having arrived at results that are perfectly clear and satisfactory
> to myself, when I try to express them in language I feel that I
> must begin by putting myself upon quite another intellectual
> plane. I have to translate my thoughts into a language that does
> not run very evenly with them. I therefore waste a vast deal of
> time in seeking for appropriate words and phrases, and am con-
> scious, when required to speak on a sudden, of being often very
> obscure through mere verbal maladroitness, and not through
> want of clearness of perception. That is one of the small an-
> noyances of my life.[8]

This Darwinian view of creativity has two interesting implications. In the first place, serendipity is not such an unusual
mental event after all. Everyone has heard the stories of serendipitous discoveries: from Archimedes' Eureka! experience
in the bathtub to Fleming's observation of the antibiotic properties of penicillin.[9] These fortuitous occasions are nothing
more than another source of blind variation. The key contrast
is whether the precipitating event comes from without rather
than from within. Moreover, those people who cerebrate the
way James described are prone to be those who make serendipitous discoveries. Paralleling the associative richness is an
openness to experience ruled by a subliminal scanning of the
outer world. This intimate link between internal and external
variations is illustrated in the scientific life of Charles Darwin
himself. His son, Francis, had ample opportunity to learn his
father's modus operandi. Charles Darwin had an impressive

instinct for arresting exceptions: it was as though he were charged with theorizing power ready to flow into any channel on the slightest disturbance, so that no fact, however small, could avoid releasing a stream of theory, and thus the fact became magnified into importance. In this way it naturally happened that many untenable theories occurred to him; but fortunately his richness of imagination was equalled by his power of judging and condemning the thoughts that occurred to him. He was just to his theories, and did not condemn them unheard; and so it happened that he was willing to test what would seem to most people not at all worth testing. These rather wild trials he called "fool's experiments," and enjoyed extremely.[10]

Obviously, a scientist so engaged has higher odds of chancing upon serendipitous discoveries.

The second implication has to do with one myth about creative genius. In the romantic conception of genius, the great intellect simply wills a creative idea into existence in a single purposive act. This notion is implied in Pope's apotheosis of Newton: "Nature and Nature's laws lay hid in night:/ God said, *Let Newton be!* and all was light." Yet according to the Darwinian model of creativity, even the most amazing creators lack this volitional power. Newton himself, when asked to explain how he came up with his monumental ideas, could only say that he pondered problems over and over. There's no shortcut around such rambling ruminations, at least not for revolutionary contributions.

Of course, once a discovery is made, and the new idea translated into a more articulate form, it may look as if the creator attained success in one fell swoop. The trials and tribulations of the thought process are left to notebooks and letters. Hermann von Helmholtz, when praised for his scientific achievements, cautioned that

the pride which I might have felt about the final result in these cases was considerably lowered by my consciousness that I had only succeeded in solving such problems after many devious ways, by the gradually increasing generalisation of favourable examples, and by a series of fortunate guesses. I had to compare myself with an Alpine climber, who, not knowing the way, ascends slowing and with toil, and is often compelled to retrace his steps because his progress is stopped; sometimes by reasoning, and sometimes by accident, he hits upon traces of a fresh path, which again leads him a little further; and finally, when he has reached the goal, he finds to his annoyance a royal road on which he might have ridden up if he had been clever enough to find the right starting-point at the outset. In my memoirs I have, of course, not given the reader an account of my wanderings, but I have described the beaten path on which he can now reach the summit without trouble.[11]

True geniuses must have the patience to relinquish their fate to the vicissitudes of chance.

I realize that this picture of the creative process bucks a fashionable trend in modern cognitive science.[12] Psychologists today often perceive creativity as a straightforward application of secondary-process thinking. The godfather of this movement is Herbert Simon—the only psychologist who has earned a Nobel Prize (albeit for economics). Simon and his colleagues are currently devising "discovery programs" that *rediscover* many laws and principles that decorate the annals of science.[13] For example, the program called BACON came up with Kepler's third law of planetary motion when given the necessary raw data. Because this computer software operates according to strictly logical rules, don't these rediscoveries disprove the Darwinian model of creativity? Not at all.

Space limitations do not permit a detailed critique of these programs, so may a few brief remarks suffice. In general, discovery programs work by applying a set of heuristics to a given set of data. The heuristics are rules of thumb that direct the computer to what may be the most profitable areas to seek a solution. In a specific problem-solving situation, however, these guidelines still must operate by a trial-and-error (or operate-and-test) procedure. Moreover, to simplify matters, discovery programs are usually endowed with a rather restricted repertoire of heuristics. In addition, the data input is severely confined. For example, to rediscover Kepler's third law the computer was given only two observations (periods of revolution and distances) for each of five planets—ten data points in all!

To make more realistic programs that handle more complex information, the supply of heuristics must be immensely enlarged. Yet as the number of heuristics expands, the heuristics themselves create a formidably large "search space." Therefore, chance will mostly determine whether you are lucky enough to have applied the optimal heuristic at the very outset of problem-solving. Moreover, often the heuristics themselves must be discovered (or created) before they can be exploited, throwing the creative process back on more primitive thought processes. Finally, of course, many problems may be too rich to yield easily to solution by any logical principle. When discussing how to discover the fundamentals of physics, Einstein warned that "to these elementary laws there leads no logical path, but only intuition."[14]

Despite these complaints, I do not want to dismiss discovery programs altogether. I have no doubt that they have captured some important processes in creativity, scientific and otherwise. Still, I argue that the logic embodied in these programs represents only one piece of a gigantic puzzle. This brings me to one final point. Researchers in the area of creativity are fond of identifying a small number of mental processes that they believe are crucial to creative genius. Thus, Albert Rothenberg pinpointed such mechanisms as homospatial and janusian imagery.[15] Silvano Arieti has demonstrated the importance of amorphous and primitive cognition.[16] Arthur Koestler underlined the impact of bisociation.[17] And so forth. Who's correct? What is the most basic process behind the creative act?

Answer: Everybody is wrong. But, like the famous proverb of the blind men and the elephant, all have captured a portion of the truth. Creativity of the highest caliber requires access to an impressive repertoire of thought processes. Seldom does "one size fit all." Instead, the creative genius must remain open to any process that works. Sometimes vivid visual imagery of some kind or another will get the job done. Other times the deliberate application of some logical principle may cut through obstacles to a solution. In other words, the mental procedures that generate new ideas are also subject to blind variation. The creator must be an opportunist, exploiting any psychological resource that succeeds. Those intellects having only one or two ways to attack problems in their field are not likely to make big names for themselves. Hence, the Darwinian perspective applies as much to mental processes as to the thoughts those processes produce. In either case, variety is the spice of creative life.[18]

PRODUCTS AND IDEAS

The creator cannot procrastinate after arriving at a fine idea. Creativity must be more than a process; it must yield a tangible product. The precise nature of this product, naturally, depends on the field of creative activity. It may be a symphony, poem, novel, painting, sculpture, architectural design, philosophical treatise, scientific journal article, or patent application and working model. Whatever the specific format, it is this concrete product that ultimately must convince appreciators, audiences, patrons, or colleagues that they have in their midst a creative genius.

Once these products have been introduced in the open market of ideas, Darwinian-style selection returns at a higher level of analysis. Instead of thoughts and processes being the units of variation and selection, the products emerging from the creator's hand provide the units. Some of the proffered products will make the grade, and receive acclaim as immortal masterpieces. Other products, even though from the same creative personality, will fail to make an impression, and will fall by the wayside as failures. The analogy here is with "reproductive success" in biological evolution. To contribute to the gene pool, you must spawn offspring. Because you cannot guarantee that all progeny will survive to maturity, it's best to have lots of descendants. Prolific reproduction heightens the odds that one or more of your brood will replicate your genes in the next generation.

This analogy helps us appreciate one exceptional feature of creative geniuses—their astonishing productivity.[19] Johann Sebastian Bach composed over a thousand pieces. That's enough pages to keep a copyist working for nearly a lifetime. Pablo Picasso signed nearly 20,000 separate compositions. Thomas Edison held 1,093 patents, still the record at the U.S. Patent Office. Einstein's bibliography contains 248 items, Freud's 330, Galton's 227. Even Charles Darwin, a virtual invalid after returning from his *Beagle* journey, claimed 119 publications at the close of his career. In fact, if you look at any field in the arts or sciences, a small elite of highly prolific creators account for most of the contributions.

This productive elitism is nicely expressed by the Price law.[20] Count the number of individuals offering their wares in an aesthetic or scientific marketplace. Then take the square root of this number. The answer tells you how many of the total have their names on *half* of all contributions. To illustrate, approximately 250 composers are credited with producing one or more compositions that are still heard in the classical repertoire. The square root of 250 is about 15.8. According to one survey, half of all classical music comes from the pens of just 16 composers,[21] a close enough congruence to prediction! Three composers alone—Mozart, Beethoven, and Bach—are responsible for nearly 20 percent of the standard repertoire. Yet this triumvirate constitutes only 1 percent of all those in the running.

With few exceptions, the most prolific contributors to a given domain are at least a hundred times more productive than their least busy colleagues.[22] Indeed, the most typical member of a creative enterprise makes but one contribution in a lifetime. As a result, those contributors who occupy the lower half of the productivity distribution account for only around 15 percent of all contributions. Significantly, these statistical statements actually understate the magnitude of productive elitism. That's because these calculations ignore all the potential contributors who begat no intellectual offspring whatsoever. All of us who teach at graduate institutions certainly have many stories to tell about stellar students who vanished into oblivion after submitting their doctoral theses. And not-withstanding the mentor's urgings, these once-promising pro-fessionals often fail even to publish their dissertations![23]

In evolutionary theory a distinction is sometimes made be-tween two kinds of reproductive strategies.[24] On the one hand, many species follow the path of *r* selection. Here organisms propagate with abandon in the blind hope that even a small percentage of their progeny will outlast all the myriad threats to their existence. This is the tactic adopted by the sea urchin. Nearly all of its seed will become mere food in the lower steps of the oceanic food pyramid. On the other hand, proportion-ally fewer species adopt the practice of *K* selection. Here the maneuver is to raise a much smaller brood, but to coax these privileged few to maturity through parental care. Birds and mammals typify this strategy. This contrast poses the critical question: Which reproductive strategy does creative output embody? Can't there exist perfectionists who confine their labors to conceiving, and nurturing to maturity, a single mag-num opus?

The response is surprising: The characteristic pattern is *r* rather than *K* selection. Empirical studies have unearthed a regularity as secure as any in the behavioral sciences, namely, the constant-probability-of-success principle.[25] This principle holds that quality is a probabilistic function of quantity. True creativity is a consequence of mere productivity. Those in-dividuals who produce the most total works will, on the av-erage, produce the most masterpieces as well. For example, the single best predictor of how often scientists are cited in the professional literature is how many publications they have to their credit.[26] Or if you wish to determine your chances of having an entry in an encyclopedia a century from now, just measure the length of the publications section of your curric-ulum vitae.[27]

In line with *r* selection, there's no evidence that the success rates are systematically higher or lower according to the size of your lifetime output. While higher productivity does not promise you success, neither are you promised the world sim-ply by doting your entire career on one ambitious project. For every perfectionist who concentrated a lifetime on a single masterpiece, there's a nonentity hidden somewhere who likewise put all the eggs in one basket, but had them crushed beneath the heels of a ruthless posterity.

If you are still among those who believe that creative geniuses have some direct and infallible conduit to truth or beauty, please disenthrall yourself! The inverse of the constant-probability-of-success principle is the constant-probability-of-failure principle. Those who boast the most hits must blush over the most misses besides. W. H. Auden stated it well: Because great poets write so much, "The chances are that, in the course of his lifetime, the major poet will write more bad poetry than the minor."[28] In a like manner, it is hard to imagine any significant creator in any domain who has not committed horrendous errors many times during his career. Not every play by Shakespeare is a masterpiece; *Timon of Athens,* for one, adds nothing to his reputation. Beethoven's status as a composer could probably do without "Wellington's Victory." Newton's efforts in alchemy are an embarrassment to his admirers. The amount of money Edison lost in devising a new method of iron ore extraction equaled all the cash he had made from the electric light bulb.

No wonder that many creators defend the value of failed experiments, overly visionary projects, and bold ventures. Einstein was one of the most monumental scientific risk-takers of all time. Yet this proclivity got him in trouble many times. He practically made a fool of himself in his attacks on quantum theory and in his formulations of the unified field theory. He justified his mistakes by claiming "Science may progress on the basis of error as long as it is not trivial." If you are going to mark your career with booboos and false starts, make them big-time! The supremely cautious will only pull off blunders of a different kind. Gauss is often seen as the archetype of the perfectionist mathematician. Despite making hundreds of contributions to mathematics and physics, he tended to sit on projects too long. The result was that he let others make discoveries that he felt not ready to publicize before his colleagues. For example, he invented a non-Euclidean geometry long before Janos Bolyai, but refused to publish the results until they met his excessively high standards. Not allowing that egg to hatch reduced Gauss's long-range impact on the pool of mathematical knowledge.

The Gauss story implies that creators are not the best judges of their work. Beethoven's favorite compositions are not always the favorites with audiences, for instance. In his own day, he thought his Moonlight Sonata was sadly overplayed, his Eighth Symphony strangely neglected. Beethoven didn't even bother to publish the bagatelle heard in almost every home that holds a piano, the *Für Elise*. Helmholtz proposed one explanation:

> My colleagues, as well as the public at large, evaluate a scientific or artistic work on the basis of its utility, its instructiveness, or the pleasure which it affords. An author is more inclined to base his evaluation on the labor a work has cost him, and it is but rarely that both kinds of judgment agree. Indeed, we can see from occasional statements of some of the most celebrated men, especially artists, that they assign small value to achievements which seem to us inimitable, compared to others which were difficult for them and yet which appear much less successful to readers and observers. I need only mention Goethe, who once said to Eckermann that he did not value his poetic works as highly as the work he had done in the theory of color.[29]

The latter effort, we now realize, was an unmitigated disaster!

Helmholtz put his finger on a crucial point. The eventual worth of a creative product does not depend on the effort the creator expended on the project. Because creativity is at bottom a hit-or-miss affair, even the greatest genius cannot attain success by some secure flash of insight or exercise of logic. For some projects, the creative individual will be lucky, and the variation–selection procedure will converge on a decent product in short order. Other works-in-progress may demand the more arduous and circuitous mental paths, with ubiquitous cul-de-sacs frustrating the quest. That Van Gogh grappled longer with his *Potato Eaters* than with *Starry Night* does not compel us to call the former the superior creation.

The principle of the constant-probability-of-success holds yet more broadly. Besides handling differences across careers in quantity and quality of output, the same principle explicates the fluctuations within an individual creator's career.[30] The ups and downs in the production of renowned masterpieces follow the same trajectory, on the average, as seen in the production of flops and trivia. Those periods in a creator's career when the best works emerge are likely to be those in which the worst appear as well. If we calculate the ratio of hits to total attempts over consecutive intervals, that proportion neither increases nor decreases with age. The odds of making a big splash are a function of the same number of times you dive, no matter how long you've been doing the sport.

The stability of the quality ratio across the life span also has an analogue in the biological world. Except in certain exceptional circumstances, such as in Down's syndrome, the adaptive fitness of the offspring is not contingent upon the age of the two parents. That is, the probability of receiving an advantageous combination of genes at the moment of conception does not vary according to the age of the progenitors who contributed the sperm and egg. That is because the Mendelian lottery yields blind variations. No matter how mature and expert the parent, the child's innate adaptive fitness is decided by the luck of the draw.

By mentioning Mendel, I am led to one concluding observation. We have assumed that the discrete product represents the level of blind variation and selective retention once a creator offers humanity some novel notion. Yet sometimes the unit of selection is not the product so much as the idea. Most creations are bundles of ideas. Occasionally some of these ideas will divorce from the product, and then struggle for existence alongside many competing ideas. This process is most apparent in the sciences. For instance, if you read Mendel's original paper on trait inheritance in peas, a curious fact emerges. The statistical analyses and theoretical arguments that became the beginnings of what we call "Mendelian genetics" form only a subsidiary part of the paper. Mendel's primary interest was in hybridization as a possible vehicle for the variation that feeds natural selection. Yet Mendel's tangential discussion acquired far greater relevance when his 1865 paper was rediscovered in 1900. His laws of trait inheritance then vied with many rival ideas about the transmission of characters from generation to generation.[31]

In the arts, too, the unit of variation may be some fragment of an aesthetic masterpiece rather than the whole entity. In the classical repertoire, for example, selections from opera—like overtures, intermezzi, preludes, and ballet numbers—will contend with genuine orchestral works for the attention of concertgoers. And a composer's labors can become even more splintered than this! Recall some commercial jingles, sound tracks, and elevator music: How often have we heard a scrap of melody from Beethoven or Tchaikovsky wrestle with another morsel from the Beatles or Scott Joplin? All the themes ever composed in the history of Western music contend to get a cut on some "album of the world's greatest hits." Again, it's time for survival of the fittest.

PERSONS AND PERSONALITIES

We have thus far sketched how the variation–selection mechanism operates on several planes—thoughts, processes, products, and ideas. Yet the unit of operation may be higher still: the creative individual. At any given point in the history of civilization, a multitude of creators compete for the attention of contemporaries and posterity. These candidates for cultural immortality represent thousands of variations on an artistic style, philosophical system, scientific paradigm, or religious worldview. In fact, empirical evidence shows that the principle of the constant-probability-of-success intrudes on the succession of generations.[32] Those periods of history that produce the most first-rate minds also tend to be those that produce the most runners-up and also-rans. Bright luminaries like Michelangelo, Beethoven, Shakespeare, Aristotle, and Pasteur each lived in times in which they were surrounded by lesser lights. Hence, the more extensive the human material to select from, the higher the odds that a certain era will attain greatness as a Golden Age.

Selection of individuals occurs in more subtle ways as well. Every creator who manages to make a mark in history can be viewed as the culmination of a long developmental process.[33] This process winnowed the geniuses from the talents, the talents from the mediocrities. Think of it this way. Each year produces a huge batch of human potential in the guise of screaming babies. Each child embodies a distinctive combination of genetic material. Sometimes a particular genetic variation holds immense promise for the generation of a future genius. Before that baby attains adulthood success, however, he or she must run the developmental gauntlet. This may require a unique confluence of environmental experiences which set the child on an innovative path.[34] For example, some circumstances favor the development of an artistic temperament, others the appearance of a scientific intellect. Thus, later-born children are more prone to become artistic creators, firstborn children to become scientific creators.[35] Similarly, artistic types are more likely to come from chaotic and diversified home environments, whereas scientific types largely emerge from stable and homogeneous settings.[36] Whether a child grows up to become an artist or scientist then requires that all the diverse factors converge on the same developmental end.

On the other hand, certain developmental influences may function after a more generic mode. That is, some conditions encourage the emergence of geniuses of all kinds.[37] For instance, being a marginal person with respect to the culture or discipline is often a tremendous asset. As Donald Campbell said, "Persons who have been uprooted from traditional cultures, or who have been thoroughly exposed to two or more cultures, seem to have an advantage in the range of hypotheses they are apt to consider, and through this means, in the frequency of creative innovation."[38] It is probably for this reason that the contribution of Jews to European civilization well exceeds their diminutive representation in the general population.

Unfortunately, the weeding of potential geniuses from the generational influx is not always rational. Social prejudices may set down inequitable requirements that deny truly capable children access to adulthood opportunities. The history of African-Americans in the United States illustrates the force of such capricious injustices well enough. And, naturally, women have had to face comparable constraints in almost every nation on the globe. Before the modern era of English literature, most of the notable females overcame these imposed obstacles by publishing anonymously or by adopting a masculine nom de plume. The first was the course taken by Jane Austen, the latter the path followed by Mary Ann Evans (George Eliot). Racism and sexism thus automatically nip certain variations in the bud.

Except for this discriminatory pruning, each human being embodies a random sampling of available genetic traits and environmental inputs. Both nature and nurture conspire in an unsystematic fashion to the making of the young adult. This aspirant for fame may or may not have what it takes to prevail in the next series of selection processes. By this point the candidate should display an exceptional intelligence, a phenomenal persistence, and an extraordinary energy—all directed toward a singular cause. The last attribute is especially pivotal. Many child prodigies fail to mature into creative geniuses precisely because they never find a distinctive goal to which they are willing to dedicate their entire lives. Genius must be *sui generis*. Yet the child prodigy often enters adulthood as a Melba-toast mediocrity. Said Will Rogers in his memoirs: "I was not a Child Prodigy, because a Child Prodigy is a child who knows as much when it is a Child as it does when it grows up."[39]

To rise above the pack of potential geniuses, a developing individual must often undergo a "crystallizing experience."[40] This is an accidental event early in childhood or adolescence that says to the talent: "*This* is what you wish to devote your whole life to." It may be a book of poetry resting on a windowsill, an exhibit at a science museum, attendance at a concert, a birthday gift, or any other seemingly chance event that sends the youth along a new course of distinction. For example,

Srinivasa Ramanujan's accidental encounter with a tutorial manual on higher mathematics deflected him from a course of provincial obscurity to international fame. Happenstances like these led Samuel Johnson to say: "The true Genius is a mind of large general powers, accidentally determined to some particular direction."[41]

Assuming that the aspirant satisfies the developmental requisites, the next step is clearly to knuckle down and produce the works that found an enduring reputation. In these arduous labors, creators must keep in mind what we learned earlier. You cannot anticipate very well whether one of your creations will be an eagle or a turkey. Therefore, to maximize your chances of election to genius status, you should pursue an optimization strategy. In the language of investment, it helps to diversify your portfolio. That is exactly what the bona-fide geniuses do. They make contributions to so many different domains, genre, media, or styles that *something* is sure to keep their name shining before posterity. Max Born said that Einstein "would be one of the greatest theoretical physicists of all times even if he had not written a single line on relativity."[42] Charles Darwin would still have become an eminent nineteenth-century biologist even if he never got around to publishing his *Origin of Species*.

It is this manifold output that enables the true creative luminaries to ride out the tides of fashion change.[43] Is Beethoven's Fifth Symphony overplayed? How about his Third or Ninth? Does Petruchio in Shakespeare's *Taming of the Shrew* come on as too sexist? Well, how about putting *As You Like It* on the boards? And if symphonies or plays are out, sonatas or sonnets might be in. The durability of posthumous reputation depends on always having something that can grab the attention of a jaded posterity. Naturally, reproductive success in the animal world is analogously promoted. That organism that produces the most offspring with the biggest variety of genetic endowments has the highest likelihood of having its progeny outlive the tests of a fickle environment.

To these considerations I'd like to add one more. When future generations make their final judgment call on a creator's life work, it's possible that their evaluations are swayed by extraneous factors. In particular, if the unit of selection is the individual, the person's life may be nearly as important as his or her work. When we get right down to it, we receive inspiration from the glorious names of the past from more than reading, hearing, or seeing their masterworks. Our enthusiasm also is elicited from reading their biographies. And some celebrities have more fascinating biographies than others. To know that someone, whose works you admire, fought through all sorts of struggles—that provides a constant source of encouragement for those of us who must also battle against the Fates.

This may explain why the biographies of famous people are so chock full of untoward happenings.[44] For example, eminent personalities are far more likely to experience parental loss in childhood or adolescence.[45] Is this because orphanhood constitutes a developmental influence that nurtures creative growth? Or is this merely one of those stigmata that gives you a special edge in the competition for the tributes of posterity? If the latter holds true, a new twist is placed on the ironic complaint of poet Dylan Thomas that "There's only one thing that's worse than having an unhappy childhood, and that's having a too-happy childhood."[46]

Admittedly, a strong case can be made that orphanhood directly nourishes the development of the creative personality. By disrupting socialization, parental loss may produce an individual capable of generating a more impressive diversity of unconventional variations. Nonetheless, other biographical tidbits do not fit so nicely into this interpretation. Take the bizarre relation between a creator's life span and posthumous fame. Those who die at unusually youthful ages, as did Keats and Shelley, often gain extra points in fame.[47] How else can we explain this except that tragic early death makes good copy?

So, are some creative geniuses wrongly neglected because they were unlikely enough to have lived boring lives? I don't have a ready answer, but I suspect that posthumous reputation is not based on a creator's body of work alone. Despite a prodigal intellect and originality, Immanuel Kant never attracted the general audience of, say, René Descartes. Kant's deplorable writing style is one culprit, no doubt. Still, his biography doesn't broaden his appeal. Spent his whole life in Königsberg, never traveling farther than fifty miles beyond its environs. He was schooled and taught at the same university. He took a daily walk so punctually that denizens could set their clocks by his footsteps. He never married. Come to think of it, Kant's life seems to prove Buffon's assertion that "the style is the man."

SCHOOLS AND CULTURES

If individuals can provide grist for the mill of variation–selection, can that Darwinian process show up at higher levels still? Can whole groups represent blind variations which are then selectively retained in consecutive generations? Does the concept of group selection found in some theories of biological evolution have a parallel in a Darwinian theory of cultural evolution? I think so.

In the sciences, creators will often subscribe to what Thomas Kuhn called a "paradigm."[48] A paradigm is a coherent set of theory and techniques that guides scientific inquiry. Often in the early stages of any scientific discipline, several paradigmatic schools will vie with each other. This competitive process works in much the same way as a variation–selection mechanism.[49] In the history of psychology, psychologists have subscribed to a diversity of paradigms. Among the most prominent are the structuralist, functionalist, behaviorist, Gestalt, psychoanalytic, Piagetian, and the cognitive schools. Whether or not a given psychologist is widely read today will hinge, in part, on the status of the school to which he or she belongs. Nowadays psychoanalysis is dying in the behavioral sciences. That means that a large number of psychologists besides Freud may find themselves disregarded as the discipline enters the next century. To distort Benjamin Franklin's well-known remark, sometimes people hang together instead of hanging separately.

In the arts, too, creators will often belong to regional schools
or movements which may or may not endure. Thus Renaissance Italy had almost as many artistic styles as it had republics
and principalities. Of this wonderful diversity, only a few,
most notably the Florentine, expanded from a provincial to a
cosmopolitan style. Florence was twice fortunate. Besides
being the land that produced Leonardo da Vinci and Michelangelo, it was the home of Dante, whose *Divine Comedy* made
Tuscan dialect the literary language of the Peninsula. The literature composed in other Italian tongues was thereby reduced
to a creative backwater.

Of course, Florence had a special advantage. Under the Med-
icis it had become an economic and political power. The Med-
icis were the bankers of Europe. Their sons became cardinals
and popes, their daughters queens. Thus, Leonardo, Michelangelo, Dante, and their compatriots had the luck to be born
at the right place at the right time. A portion of their creative
accomplishments may be ascribed to their having become the
ornaments of economic and political leaders. Nor is this exceptional. The achievements of hundreds of creators often rise
or fall with the extrinsic pulsations of the material world.
England beats out Portugal in building a colonial empire, and
so Milton's *Paradise Lost* becomes more widely read than *The
Lusiads* of Camoëns. Communism hit the dust in Europe, suddenly making both socialist realism and Marxist criticism ir-
revocably passé. Too often, perhaps, the merits of individual
creators turn not on the quality of their best works or the
example of their lives, but on the caprice of power.

Yet however much we may lament the reality, this whimsy
does not contradict a Darwinian perspective. The extinction
of life forms is not always determined by the pure adaptive
fitness of a species. Ocean levels may change, precipitation
patterns alter, local ecologies shift, and volcanoes erupt—all
without the tiniest regard for the intrinsic merits of the organisms that occupy an unlucky niche. The indiscriminate
havoc wreaked by asteroids on our planet's protoplasmic blan-
ket compares with the unprecedented destruction heaped on
the civilizations of the New World by the Spanish conquis-

tadors. Who can imagine the masterpieces that might have emerged had that evolutionary progression not been so ruthlessly terminated! Would there have arisen an Aztec Homer, an Incan Phidias, even a Mayan Ptolemy?

Our speculations may rise to the cosmic. Very likely, intelligent life exists elsewhere in our galaxy. On some of these planets, civilizations have emerged with their own creators of genius. If the fantasy of science fiction is one day realized, and these hitherto isolated cultures begin to exchange ideas, Darwinian variation and selection will operate on a yet higher plane. Each planetary civilization will represent but one realization of an infinite number of potential biological and cultural evolutions. In that struggle for supremacy, we have no assurance that Earth's achievements will fare well. Perhaps names like Copernicus, Descartes, Shakespeare, Tolstoy, Beethoven, and Michelangelo will be tossed on the dust heap of galactic evolution—the victims of group selection more grandiose than anything so far witnessed. Who knows? If afterward the galaxies of the cosmos begin to communicate and compete, what then? And what of galaxy clusters?

This essay by no means exhausts what can be said on this topic. Indeed, the documentation presented here is practically a random sample of all the points that might be made on behalf of the Darwinian view of creativity. Whole books have been published that extend Donald Campbell's blind-variation and selective-retention model to various facets of creative genius.[50] To offer a hint of the possible applications, these more extensive discussions show how the model can explain (1) the impact of certain variables on creative development, (2) the personality profile of creative geniuses, (3) the age curves for creative output, (4) the occurrence of multiple discoveries and inventions, and (5) the evolutionary shifts in literary, artistic, and musical styles. At the same time, a detailed account would have to punctuate the speculative fancy with several critical caveats. Primary among these is this: We should not expect intimate parallels between biological and cultural evolution.

Any attempt to draw detailed correspondences between evolution by natural selection and evolution by cultural selection is doomed to fail. There are just too many contrasts between the nitty-gritty of chromosomes and organisms, on the one hand, and thoughts and societies, on the other. Nevertheless, the Darwinian perspective does capture a generic model of unusual explanatory breadth.

The Darwinian viewpoint even applies to what I am doing this very second. After generating sundry ideas when I first sat down to type this paper, I have selected a tiny subset for presentation here. The final draft of this essay hereby enters a new level of variation and selection. As one article among millions, it must compete with all the rival accounts of the creative process. Yet even were I a Darwin, I would have not power to forecast whether this or any other contribution will survive to add luster to my name generations hence. But happily for my personal prospects, these pages are only a few leaves out of whole reams that I have so far thrust before the curious. So perhaps something in my hand is bound to bear intellectual progeny. If not, that ignominious occurrence will be because either I or the Western culture which bred me did not make the next cut in the Darwinian editing of ideas.

NOTES

1. Dean Keith Simonton, "Creativity, Leadership, and Chance," in *The Nature of Creativity,* edited by R. J. Sternberg (New York: Cambridge University Press), pp. 386–486.
2. Donald T. Campbell, "Blind Variation and Selective Retention in Creative Thought as in Other Knowledge Processes," *Psychological Review,* 67 (1960):380–400.
3. John Dryden, "Epistle Dedicatory of The Rival Ladies," in *Essays of John Dryden,* edited by W. P. Ker (Oxford: Clarendon Press, 1926), Vol. 1, p. 1.
4. Jacques Hadamard, *An Essay on the Psychology of Invention in the Mathematical Field* (Princeton, NJ: Princeton University Press, 1945), p. 30.

5. William James, "Great Men, Great Thoughts, and the Environment," *Atlantic Monthly*, 46 (1880):456.
6. Hadamard, *Psychology of Invention*, p. 28.
7. Ibid., p. 142.
8. Ibid., p. 69.
9. Walter W. Cannon, "The Role of Chance in Discovery," *Scientific Monthly*, 50 (1940):204–209.
10. Francis Darwin (Ed.), *The Autobiography of Charles Darwin and Selected Letters* (New York: Dover, 1958), p. 101.
11. Hermann von Helmholtz, "An Autobiographical Sketch," in *Popular Lectures on Scientific Subjects, Second Series*, translated by E. Atkinson (New York: Longman, Green, 1898), p. 282.
12. Margaret Boden, *The Creative Mind* (New York: Basic Books, 1990). Robert W. Weisberg, *Creativity* (New York: Freeman, 1986).
13. Pat Langley, Herbert A. Simon, Gary L. Bradshaw, & Jan M. Zytkow, *Scientific Discovery* (Cambridge, MA: MIT Press, 1987).
14. Gerald Holton, "On Trying to Understand the Scientific Genius," *American Scholar*, 41 (1971–1972):97.
15. Albert Rothenberg, *The Emerging Goddess* (Chicago: University of Chicago Press, 1979).
16. Silvano Arieti, *The Magic Synthesis* (New York: Basic Books, 1976).
17. Arthur Koestler, *The Act of Creation* (New York: Dell, 1964).
18. Robert Scott Root-Bernstein, *Discovering* (Cambridge, MA: Harvard University Press, 1989).
19. Dean Keith Simonton, *Genius, Creativity, and Leadership* (Cambridge, MA: Harvard University Press, 1984), Ch. 5.
20. Derek J. de Solla Price, *Little Science, Big Science* (New York: Columbia University Press, 1963), Ch. 2.
21. Abraham Moles, *Information Theory and Aesthetic Perception*, translated by J. E. Cohen (Urbana: University of Illinois Press, 1958).
22. Wayne Dennis, "Variations in Productivity among Creative Workers," *Scientific Monthly*, 80 (1955):277–278.
23. Benjamin S. Bloom, "Report on Creativity Research by the Examiner's Office of the University of Chicago," in *Scientific Creativity*, edited by C. W. Taylor & F. Barron (New York: Wiley, 1963), pp. 251–264.
24. Edward O. Wilson, *Sociobiology* (Cambridge, MA: Harvard University Press, 1975).

25. Dean Keith Simonton, "Creative Productivity, Age, and Stress: A Biographical Time-Series Analysis of 10 Classical Composers," *Journal of Personality and Social Psychology,* 35 (1977):791–804. Dean Keith Simonton, "Quality, Quantity, and Age: The Careers of 10 Distinguished Psychologists," *International Journal of Aging and Human Development,* 21 (1985):241–254.

26. Jonathan R. Cole & Stephen Cole, *Social Stratification in Science* (Chicago: University of Chicago Press, 1973). Dean Keith Simonton, "Leaders of American Psychology, 1879–1967: Career Development, Creative Output, and Professional Achievement," *Journal of Personality and Social Psychology,* 62 (1992):1–13.

27. Wayne Dennis, "Bibliographies of Eminent Scientists," *Scientific Monthly,* 80 (1954):180–183.

28. William Bennett, "Providing for Posterity," *Harvard Magazine,* 82, No. 3 (1980):15.

29. Russell Kahl (Ed.), *Selected Writings of Hermann von Helmholtz* (Middletown, CT: Wesleyan University Press, 1971), p. 467.

30. Dean Keith Simonton, "Age and Outstanding Achievement: What Do We Know after a Century of Research?" *Psychological Bulletin,* 104 (1988):251–267.

31. Augustine Brannigan, "The Reification of Mendel," *Social Studies of Science,* 9 (1979):423–454.

32. Dean Keith Simonton, "Artistic Creativity and Interpersonal Relationships Across and Within Generations," *Journal of Personality and Social Psychology,* 46 (1984):1273–1286. Dean Keith Simonton, "Galtonian Genius, Kroeberian Configurations, and Emulation: A Generational Time-Series Analysis of Chinese Civilization," *Journal of Personality and Social Psychology,* 55 (1988):230–238.

33. Death Keith Simonton, "Developmental Antecedents of Achieved Eminence," *Annals of Child Development,* 5 (1987):131–169.

34. Mihaly Csikszentmihalyi & Rick E. Robinson, "Culture, Time, and the Development of Talent," in *Conceptions of Giftedness,* edited by R. J. Sternberg & J. E. Davidson (New York: Cambridge University Press, 1986), pp. 264–284.

35. Anne Roe, *The Making of a Scientist* (New York: Dodd, Mead, 1952). William D. Bliss, "Birth of Creative Writers," *Journal of Individual Psychology,* 26 (1970):200–202.

36. Charles E. Schaefer & Anne Anastasi, "A Biographical Inven-

tory for Identifying Creativity in Adolescent Boys," *Journal of Applied Psychology,* 58 (1968):42–48.

37. Dean Keith Simonton, "Biographical Typicality, Eminence, and Achievement Style," *Journal of Creative Behavior,* 20 (1986):14–22.

38. Campbell, "Selective Retention in Creative Thought," p. 391.

39. Donald Day (Ed.), *The Autobiography of Will Rogers* (Boston: Houghton Mifflin, 1949), p. 4.

40. Joseph Walters & Howard Gardner, "The Crystallizing Experience: Discovering an Intellectual Gift," in *Conceptions of Giftedness,* edited by R. J. Sternberg & J. E. Davidson (New York: Cambridge University Press, 1986), pp. 306–331.

41. Samuel Johnson, *The Lives of the Most Eminent English Poets* (London: Bathurst et al., 1781), Vol. 1, p. 5.

42. Banesh Hoffmann, *Albert Einstein* (New York: Plume, 1972), p. 7.

43. Dean Keith Simonton, "Philosophical Eminence, Beliefs, and Zeitgeist: An Individual-Generational Analysis," *Journal of Personality and Social Psychology,* 34 (1976):630–640. Dean Keith Simonton, "Latent-Variable Models of Posthumous Reputation: A Quest for Galton's G," *Journal of Personality and Social Psychology,* 60 (1991):607–619.

44. Victor Goertzel & Mildred George Goertzel, *Cradles of Eminence* (Boston: Little, Brown, 1962).

45. J. Marvin Eisenstadt, "Parental Loss and Genius," *American Psychologist,* 33 (1978):211–223.

46. Paul Ferris, *Dylan Thomas* (London: Hodder & Stoughton, 1977), p. 49.

47. Dean Keith Simonton, *Psychology, Science, and History* (New Haven, CT: Yale University Press, 1987), pp. 135–136.

48. Thomas Kuhn, *Structure of Scientific Revolutions,* 2nd ed. (Chicago: University of Chicago Press, 1970).

49. David L. Hull, *Science as a Process* (Chicago: University of Chicago Press, 1988).

50. Colin Martindale, *The Clockwork Muse* (New York: Basic Books, 1990). Dean Keith Simonton, *Scientific Genius* (New York: Cambridge University Press, 1988).

CREATIVITY AND THE QUANTUM SELF

DANAH ZOHAR

IN OUR EVERYDAY thoughts about creativity, we tend to think of it in two senses. We sometimes mean the kind of creativity that we see around us in the natural and living world, the simple but awe-inspiring creativity associated with birth, or with the birth of stars and galaxies, the birth of new particles in the quantum laboratory. At other times we mean the kind of full-blown, purposive creativity of the human mind, the kind of creativity that gives us art, music, literature, and science. I want to argue that these two senses of creativity are inextricably linked.

I am going to concentrate on the creativity of the conscious human mind, but in doing so I want to argue that we can see the origins of that creativity in the same principles and processes that underlie the creativity of the physical and biological worlds. I want to suggest, in short, that human consciousness is a phenomenon of the physical world and that we can usefully talk about a physics of mind, or a physics of consciousness. I think we can link that physics of the mind to our natural capacity for creativity. More strongly than that, I think that if we understand this physics of our minds, understand the laws and principles that drive us to be what we are, we can both understand ourselves better and through that understanding enhance our own creative powers.

In suggesting that human consciousness is part and parcel of the physical world, I am adopting what for some people is a very controversial position. There is a long tradition in the

West of seeing consciousness as separate from the physical world. This dualist tradition goes back at least as far as Plato, who separated his realm of Forms or Ideas from the realm of experience. Christianity took this same split between mind and its experience in the world further by claiming that the human soul is a spark of the Divine. The Christian soul is something given to us by our Creator, and is wholly other from the base matter of which our bodies are created. In more modern times, Descartes set the seal on this tradition with his famous distinction between mind and body. "I rightly conclude," he said,

> . . . that my essence consists in this alone, that I am a thinking thing. . . . And although perhaps I have a body with which I am closely conjoined, I have on the one hand a clear and distinct idea of my self as a thinking, non-extended thing; it is therefore certain that I am truly distinct from my body, and can exist without it.[1]

For dualists like Descartes, the capacity for creativity in human beings was one of the clear proofs that the mind, or the soul, was part of some higher reality and was completely distinct from the base physical world.

In the seventeenth century, following Descartes' sharp split between the mental and the physical, Isaac Newton clarified in a new way the nature of the physical world. Newton's new material world was as mindless and as soulless as Descartes could have wished. Newtonian matter is lifeless. It is nonteleological, or without purpose, and it is utterly deterministic. In Newtonian physics things happen because there are fixed laws that make them happen. B will always follow A in the same predictable way.

Newtonian physics is reductionist. That is, any composite of matter can always be broken down into the sum of its parts and the forces interacting between those parts. We can always say, "This system is made of A plus B plus the forces acting between them." And Newtonian matter is also noncreative. Nothing really surprising ever happens in Newton's world.

Everything is predicted by the determinist laws linking all systems and their subparts; everything is laid down, as it were, in a grand blueprint. We may *experience* surprise, as with chaotic systems, because we were ignorant about the initial conditions of a system, or ignorant of all the parts involved and the forces acting between them, but once this ignorance is removed, we will say, "Ah, yes, that had to happen."

I believe that Newton's view of matter has touched us all very deeply, even those who are largely ignorant of physics. In our everyday perception of ourselves and our world we still live to a very large extent within the Newtonian worldview. This has produced two quite different reactions in people. Some needed to make a sharp distinction between themselves and the world of Newtonian matter. They wanted to see themselves as wholly other than determinist, causal, nonteleological brute matter, as something unique and apart. But this view tears human beings out from the fabric of the universe around us and leads to a terrible sense of alienation. We become a meaningless and helpless afterthought in a world that was otherwise rigorously planned. Bertrand Russell summed up this alienation at the turn of the century. "The world that science gives us for our belief," he wrote,

> . . . tells us that Man is the product of causes that had no prevision of the end they were achieving. That his origin, his growth, his hopes and fears, his loves and his beliefs, are but the outcome of accidental collocations of atoms. That no fire, no heroism, no intensity of thought and feeling, can preserve the individual life beyond the grave. That all the labours of the ages, all the devotion, all the inspiration, all the noon-day brightness of human genius, are destined to extinction in the vast death of the solar system, and the whole temple of Man's achievement must inevitably be buried beneath the debris of a universe in ruins.[2]

I think that the sense of despair to which such alienation gives rise remains with many of us still today, a sense of despair in the face of an overdetermined, noncreative, and ultimately meaningless physical world that fails to include us.

But there was also another, radically opposite reaction to Newton's picture of physical reality. Instead of saying, "We're different, we're special, we're set apart from all this meaningless determinism," some thinkers took the whole Newtonian worldview on board as applying to human beings as well. These people looked to Newton's work as a model for how to structure our picture of human behavior and human potential. This model has come down to most of us most directly through its impact on Freud's work.

Freud was very impressed with Newton's achievement and he wanted to emulate in psychology what Newton had done in physics. Freud wanted to discover the laws and principles of the psyche that would mirror those same laws and principles in physics and chemistry. He saw the psyche as a vast hydraulic system, where the push and pull of instinctive forces—the forces associated with sex and aggression—would determine how the system would behave. As a result, Freud had difficulty accounting for any notion of human creativity. Creativity didn't sit well with his picture of a highly determined, force-driven, instinctive psyche.

After Freud, the Behaviorists went further still. They, too, based their model of human behavior on Newton's view of determinist matter related through causal connections. With their theory of stimulus and response, they arrived at the notion that we are just so many Pavlovian dogs. If *A* happens, we will react in a certain way; if *B,* then we will react in another, equally predictable, way.

Both the Freudian and the Behaviorist views of a determinist self got taken up into our sense of what we are. They spilled over into legal and sociological theory, where it was assumed that all behavior could be explained in terms of a person's past, his gene pool, or his childhood experience. It is quite common for defense lawyers to argue that their client was a hapless victim of circumstance, a person who "had" to commit a certain crime because that crime was the predictable response to past circumstances. Such thinking takes away all sense of our free will or our responsibility for our actions.

More recently still, the artificial intelligence (AI) lobby has adopted this same mechanistic model. According to AI, we are just like our word processors. It is as though we have so many silicon chips rattling around inside our heads. Again, this is a very causal and determinist view of the human mind. It is a very noncreative view. AI can account for how we do rote activities, but it cannot account for how we ever do anything new. It can't account for the invention of new language or new concepts. My word processor never does anything that I don't tell it to do—except have accidents and breakdowns! It never comes up with anything positive that I haven't programmed into it. It can't create.

I believe quite firmly that we are right to see ourselves as physical creatures. I think that we are right to see ourselves and our minds, to see all our noblest qualities, as part and parcel of the physical world around us. But I think that those people who have turned to Newtonian physics for their model of human behavior have got the wrong physics. Newtonian physics is no longer the physics of our times. It is not the physics of creativity and complexity and self-organizing systems.

I think that to understand the creative aspects of the human mind we must turn to quantum physics. This "new" physics has been around for some seventy years, though it is only just beginning to permeate the popular consciousness. We are only just beginning to see that there is something about this physics that touches us, that tells us something interesting about ourselves.

Quantum physics is very different from Newtonian physics in several very important ways that bear on the subject of creativity.

For one thing, as we have seen, Newtonian physics is determinate. Things happen in a particular way because the rules of the game say they have to happen in that way. Nothing surprising ever happens.* Quantum systems, however, are in-

*Except in chaotic systems, but there the surprise arises from our ignorance of the way the system will unfold simply because that unfolding is too rapid and too complex for viable prediction. Chaotic systems are just as determinate as any other Newtonian system.

determinate. We can't look at a quantum system and say, "Ah yes, this is where the system begins and these are the rules of its unfolding and therefore we know it will end up there."

There is nothing that *has* to happen with an unfolding quantum system. These systems are probabilistic at best. We can *guess* how the system will unfold on the basis of the probabilities, but we may at any time be proved wrong. There is always the element of indeterminacy, and hence always an element of surprise. Genuinely new things may happen at any time.

Second, the world of Newtonian physics is a world of single reality. Newtonian systems are as they seem and can always be described exactly with a single set of parameters. Quantum physics, on the other hand, is a world of multiple realities—all superimposed one upon the other and often even mutually contradictory. The Schrödinger equation that describes the quantum realm is a celebration of rich diversity. It contains within itself an infinite spread of potentialities, none of which can be thoroughly pinned down or described exactly (Heisenberg's uncertainty principle).

The best-known instance of quantum multiple reality is the so-called wave/particle duality. In Newtonian physics, the constituents of matter are *either* particles *or* waves. In quantum reality, things are *both* waves *and* particles, simultaneously. Quantum "bits" have a dual aspect, a wave aspect and a particle aspect, both equally real and equally primary, and both coexisting at the same time.

Another important difference between Newtonian physics and the world of quantum reality springs from their different relations to causality. Newton's world is a rigidly causal world. Things happen because they are *made* to happen. *A* pushes *B*, *B* pulls *A,* etc. Quantum events, by contrast, are often acausal. They just happen as they happen. They also happen in eerie correlations, or "nonlocal" relationships.

If two photons, for instance, are shot out of a source in different directions, toward opposite ends of a room, we find that their polarities, when measured, always end up opposite to each other. No force or signal passes between them. Nothing tells one what the other is doing. Yet each behaves as though the two of them are linked across space and time as inseparable parts of some larger whole. This correlation can happen even if the photons are on opposite sides of the universe.

This "nonlocality," as the correlations are called, has a direct bearing on our search for the physical roots of creativity. It is linked directly to how new things emerge at the quantum level.

In Newtonian physics, when two atoms or particles meet, they bump into and clash with each other. Newtonian particles are like billiard balls. They are "hard," impenetrable. They never get inside each other, they are never defined in terms of each other. But quantum nonlocality is about a radically different, more creative kind of meeting.

When quantum systems meet, their wave aspects overlap and combine—just like the waves that we can see meeting on the surface of a pond. Because these quantum waves are in an indeterminate state, their properties can get into nonlocal correlation, and when they do, new properties emerge. When two quantum systems meet, they become parts of a larger whole, parts of a new system with its own unique, emergent properties. This new quantum whole cannot be reduced to the sum of its parts. Some of its properties have come into being through relationship. They could not have been predicted and they cannot be reduced. They are radically creative.

I have mentioned briefly three or four characteristics of quantum reality that are more akin to creative processes than are their Newtonian counterparts. But what has creativity in the quantum domain got to do with us? How can emergent quantum realities have any bearing on the roots of human creativity? To answer these questions, I want to turn to a discussion of the possible quantum origins of human consciousness.

There are several very good phenomenological reasons for suspecting that the physical basis of our conscious life is quantum mechanical rather than Newtonian. That is, we can look at several features of our conscious life and see these same features mirrored in the properties of quantum reality.

There is, for instance, the mysterious unity of consciousness. As I sit in this room, I am at every moment bombarded by billions of sensory data—tactile, auditory, visual, olfactory, etc. Yet I don't perceive the room in billions of fragments. I perceive it all of a piece, as a unity. But if consciousness arises, as the AI people say, from the stimulation of the 10^{11} neurons in my brain, from whence comes this unity?

The unity of consciousness troubled Descartes, and was one of his main philosophical reasons for believing that mind and body must be different. "There is a great difference between mind and body," he said, "inasmuch as the body is by its very nature always divisible, while the mind is utterly indivisible." But Descartes was of course thinking of bodies in reductionist, Newtonian terms, as things which can always be broken down into their separate parts. Quantum physical reality is very different. Here the "parts" of reality overlap and combine to form an irreducible whole. Quantum reality has what the physicist David Bohm calls a quality of "unbroken wholeness." It possesses the same unity characteristic of our mental processes.

Similar to the unity of consciousness is the unity of agency, or the unity of the person. Where do "I" come from? How can I account for my psychological integrity? Again, with a Newtonian physical model, I can't. On a Newtonian view, "I" can always be reduced to a fiction, an illusory sum of many reducible parts. But on a quantum view we have a physical basis for seeing "I" as an emergent, holistic phenomenon.

Again, we must consider free will and the potentials of human imagination. We perceive ourselves as free, we feel that we do make decisions and that we are responsible for our actions. We may at times be tempted by the determinist view that everything is caused to happen—by our genetic inheritance or our past experience—but in our deepest intuitions we know that that is not true. We are free agents. But where can we find the physical correlate of this freedom?

In Newtonian physics, we have seen that everything is deterministic. No Newtonian system in the brain could give consciousness its property of freedom. But a quantum physical system could. Quantum indeterminacy just might underlie our own capacity to make decisions and to bear responsibility.

With our imaginations, we can visualize all sorts of possibilities, and all at once. Sometimes these possibilities contradict each other and yet we can hold them in our minds simultaneously. Now in Newtonian physics we have seen that there can be only one reality at a time. Newton's world is not a world of potential or of contradictory coexistence. But we have seen that the Schrödinger wave equation is a rich celebration of diversity. Within the quantum wave function many possibilities do coexist; they coexist in superpositions like the wave/particle dualism of light.

When quantum systems evolve, they do so much like our own thoughts evolve in the realm of the imagination. We "play" with ideas, we "throw out feelers" to see how a possible scenario sits with us. Quantum systems do exactly the same thing. A many-possibilitied quantum system throws out feelers toward the future to see what its most stable next state might be. These feelers are called "virtual transitions." They are thrown out many at a time, in all directions at once. And though these transitions are only "virtual," they can and do have *real* effects in the world, just as the thoughts we entertain in imagination often have real consequences for our behavior and relationships.

I believe that in the testing nature of our imaginations we are behaving exactly like quantum systems throwing out their feelers toward the future. Our capacity for creativity, I think, is linked to similar processes in the brain, and to their quantum underpinnings. The fact that we can form new concepts, new ideas, new artistic creations, new linguistic structures is all I believe founded on the essential creativity of quantum systems. It is founded on their ability to "imagine" different futures and on their ability to form new emergent wholes as a result of their explorations.

And finally, there is one more very good reason for suspecting that our brains may include a quantum mechanical system. This is that quantum phenomena with the properties we have just discussed have been found in biological tissue.

Many people have thought that the tantalizing analogies between quantum processes and our own thought processes would suggest a quantum basis to consciousness, but the temperature of the brain has always seemed an insuperable problem. The kinds of quantum systems with the necessary properties of coherence are usually found only in very hot systems (laser beams) or in very cold systems (superfluids and superconductors). The brain, on the other hand, is warm and sticky. But since the 1960s several hundred experimental research papers have verified the existence of body-temperature quantum effects in biological tissue. Such effects were theoretically predicted by Professor Herbert Fröhlich at England's Liverpool University.[3]

I want just for a moment to discuss what a quantum brain model might look like, how it might actually function. My purpose is just to give a concrete image of the kinds of phenomena that might underlie our conscious lives so that we can then go on to see how these are linked to the physical roots of our creative processes.

In the standard AI brain model, in which we are thought to be sophisticated versions of our own word processors, the emphasis is put on the brain's 10^{11} neurons and the junctions between them. Our mental functions are thought to arise from electrochemical signals traveling along the neurons and passing information signals at the junctions, the synapses. Few AI people worry about the problem of consciousness, but if it is accepted that there is such a phenomenon, then it, too, must in some way arise from synapse activity.

A quantum brain model is concerned with quite a different level of brain activity. Neurons as a whole are too large to get into the kind of correlated relationships necessary to produce quantum effects. So if we are looking for such quantum effects, we must go down a level. In Fröhlich's work on quantum effects in biological tissue, the focus of attention is on molecules in the cell membranes. In the brain, these would be molecules lining the neuron cell membranes (or perhaps ion channels in the dendritic spines).

In every cell membrane, the molecules lining the membrane are charged dipoles. That is, they are positive at one end and negative at the other. When electrochemical energy generated by sensory stimuli passes through the cell, it causes these electric dipoles to vibrate, emitting tiny microwave "radio" signals as they do so. What Fröhlich predicted, and what has since been proved, is that at a critical threshold of energy (which varies from system to system), these dipoles all begin to vibrate in unison, so that the microwave signals they produce get pulled into a coherent microwave field. This coherent field has all the characteristics of quantum coherence.

If we are looking for the physical origins of quantum phenomena in the brain, I believe the Fröhlich work is a good place to start. It does at least show that a coherent quantum field phenomenon stretching over large portions of the brain is *feasible*. Such a coherent field, itself an emergent phenomenon not reducible to the various jiggling molecules that produce it, could pull all the diverse bits of sensory data bombarding the brain into a unified, coherent whole, thus accounting for the noted unity of consciousness and unity of the person.

There is as yet no experimental evidence for the existence of Fröhlich systems or their like in brain tissue. But it is tempting to believe that if coherent quantum phenomena are found in water at room temperature,[4] in yeast cells,[5] and in more complex biological tissue,[6] they are most likely present in the brain's neural tissue as well. If so, they might provide the ideal physical basis for the observed characteristics of consciousness. It is certainly the case that neurobiologists now know that coherent neural oscillations in large sections of the brain integrate sensory experience.[7]

If we accept that the brain has a quantum physical system linked to the emergence of consciousness, the overall brain model that we adopt would have two linked systems which together could account for our mental life. In a digital system, we would find all the neural activity so beloved of AI. This system would account for the *structure* of consciousness, for our capacity to analyze data and to digest information. The fact that we humans have larger frontal lobes, possessing more of this neural activity, would account for our greater capacity for such data processing.

But working in tandem with the digital system, I am suggesting there is also a quantum substrate. This substrate would work to pull all our available data into a coherent conscious field, giving us the capacity to see our experience as a unity. It would also give me the capacity to experience myself as a unity, as an "I" emergent from all my brain activity.

It is necessary now to introduce just one technical term, because it is essential to linking the structure of consciousness with the roots of creativity in the physical universe. The kind of quantum system that I have just described as existing in biological tissue—and possibly in the brain—is called a "Bose–Einstein condensate."[8] It was named after Einstein and the Indian physicist Bose because they were the first to describe the unique properties of this kind of physical structure.

A Bose–Einstein condensate has two distinctive properties. It is both incredibly coherent (behaves all of a piece) and incredibly unified. It is so unified that the many molecules in such a condensate behave as though they are all just one big molecule. Every part of it is overlapped and combined with every other part so that they all share the same space and time. All the parts are pulled into one holistic system.

A laser beam is a reasonably familiar Bose–Einstein condensate, and that is why laser beams can generate such remarkably coherent light. The various photons in the beam have become so overlapped and combined that it is as though they are all just one photon. There is no interference, no friction, no "noise." Superfluids and superconductors are also Bose–Einstein condensates.

The important thing for our purposes about Bose–Einstein condensates, apart from their possible link with consciousness, is that they are made out of "bosons." Despite all the many variations, all the particles in the universe come in only two basic sorts—fermions and bosons. Fermions are, if you like, particles of matter. They are things we can feel and touch. Tables and chairs and bodies are made out of fermions. It is an important property of fermions that they are a bit "antisocial." They don't like getting too close to one another. They push each other away. That is why matter doesn't collapse in on itself.

Bosons, on the other hand, are particles of relationship. All the fundamental forces in the universe, the strong and weak nuclear forces, the electromagnetic force, and the gravitational force, are made out of bosons. These are the forces that bind the universe together. They do so because bosons are essentially "social." They like being close to one another. They naturally draw together.

In suggesting that consciousness arises from a Bose–Einstein condensate in the brain, I am suggesting that an important property of our mental life is itself a boson force field. This tells us that we have a particular place in the universe, that we are intimately linked with other boson force fields, with the force fields that bind the universe together. I think this insight is crucial for understanding both the physical origins and the nature of our creativity. It can help us to trace the roots of our own creative processes back to the earliest origins of the physical universe.

We can see the essentially creative nature of even the simplest of bosons by considering an experiment done on photons— particles of light, that is, particles of electromagnetic energy. This experiment is called a photon-bunching experiment. A source emits photons in a stream, one at a time. To be very simple, let us imagine that the source emits one photon every second. After they are emitted, the photons travel a certain distance and then hit a screen, where they are registered.

Common sense would lead us to expect that one photon would hit the detecting screen each second. But that is not what happens. Instead, the photons bunch together. They cling to one another in sticky little clusters and arrive at the screen in crowds. In each of these bunches, because their wave aspects have overlapped and combined, the photons become parts of emergent wholes, parts of new realities.

I think that in the example of this photon bunching we can see the origins of both consciousness and creativity in the universe. Photons are bosons, and presumably all other bosons would behave the same. They would seek each other out and in their meeting create new emergent realities. I believe that in this experiment we are seeing the "great-great-grandfather" of the boson condensation that may well give us the physical basis of human consciousness.

Photon bunching, or its like, is but the first stage of a long chain of increasingly complex creative processes that give rise to emergent realities in the physical world. At a further stage of creativity, we have Ilya Prigogine's "open-dynamic systems," or self-organizing systems.[9] These self-organizing systems soak up chaos from the environment around them and pull it into a structured, dynamic pattern.

The simplest self-organizing system, with which we are all familiar, is a whirlpool like that that we see in our bathroom basins each morning. It takes water molecules from the surrounding fluid and pulls them into a tight, dynamical pattern. The individual molecules within the whirlpool are different at every moment, but their dynamical pattern of self-organization persists. It creates order out of chaos. In doing so, it seems to violate the second law of thermodynamics (entropy).

Prigogine has suggested that life is such a dynamical self-organizing system, that life has the capacity to defeat chaos and entropy because of its capacity for creative self-organization. I would like to take this one step further and suggest that living systems must be *quantum mechanical* self-organizing systems. I suggest this because life isn't just ordered. It is also coherent. Living systems are all of a piece, they are holistic, they are greater than the sum of their parts. We need self-organizing dynamics to get the order of living systems, we need quantum mechanics to get their coherence.

I believe that human consciousness, with all its creative potential, is just this—an incredibly complex, quantum mechanical, self-organizing system. The products of consciousness, our concepts, our art, our moral vision, are the coherent patterns that this system *can't help* generating, just as the whirlpool can't help generating its ordered pattern.

I want, for a moment, to tie up another important feature of Prigogine's creative self-organizing systems with something that is often said about human creativity. We know that madness and creativity seem to be linked. People prone to, but not quite ruined by, manic-depression are among our species' most creative people. They seem to live on a precipice between order and chaos, their work inspired by the kind of creative tension this generates. Prigogine's self-organizing systems, too, exist at such a precipice. They exist at what he calls "far from equilibrium conditions,"[10] delicately poised between order and chaos. This poise gives them an *impulse to create order.*

I believe that all of us live on this creative brink between order and chaos. This follows not from our all being manic-depressives but from the more basic physics of our consciousness. The conscious mind can't help forming creative, self-organizing patterns from the material in its environment.

Like the photons that can't help bunching, and the whirlpools that can't help ordering the chaos around them, we can't help but take the disparate information that bombards our brains at every moment and turn it into an ordered, coherent whole. There is, as Prigogine has pointed out, an arrow of time in all self-organizing systems. They *must* go forward, from chaos to order.

I want now to finish with a brief second look at the link between human imagination and quantum multiple reality. I think this, too, has a direct bearing on the roots and dynamic of our creative processes.

I think it would be useful to introduce Schrödinger's cat[11] at this point. Schrödinger's cat is a quantum cat, and thus he has special quantum abilities that make his life story interesting. This cat is kept in an opaque box. No one can see inside. In the box with the cat is a source of good food, a source of deadly poison, and a radioactive device that will randomly trigger the release of either the food or the poison.

In the world of common sense, we would expect that either the radioactive source triggers the poison, and the cat dies, or else it triggers the food and the cat lives on to purr contentedly. But because this is a quantum situation, with a quantum cat, all things are possible, simultaneously. So in fact, Schrödinger's cat eats both the poison and the food, and he is both dead and alive, at the same time. He exists in a quantum superposition of both states.

The cat only becomes dead *or* alive when we open the box

and look at him. Nobody knows why this is, but we do know that the act of looking at a quantum system, the act of measuring it, changes many-possibilitied quantum reality into mundane, daily, either/or actuality.

I think that in our conscious minds we play both roles in this story, and that the playing of these roles is necessary to the dynamics of creativity. With our imaginations, we are all like Schrödinger's cat. We dwell in a world of multiple, often even contradictory, possibilities. This is the source of our creative potential. But when we focus on our imaginary musings, when we take our fuzzy, multiple pre-thoughts and turn them into clear, focused thoughts, we pluck one of those many possibilities out and actualize it. At this stage, we lose touch with all the other potentials. We are thrust into the world of everyday, singular reality.

Artists, writers, and musicians go through this process all the time. They dwell in the world of multiple possibility through the gift of rich imagination. But when they focus on their work, when they actualize it, they lose sight of the multiple possibilities. This is why it is often destructive for a writer to talk about, or to structure too tightly, his work before he does it. The artist can never work to a blueprint.

I believe we can understand the dynamics of this creative process through the actual physics of consciousness. When we are unfocused, our minds are in a dreamy, low-energy state. Our thoughts can then exist in a quantum superposition. We can be "alive and dead" at the same time. But when we concentrate, energy flows through the brain. This energy, like the measurement process in the quantum laboratory, collapses the wavefunction of thought. That is, it turns our many-possibilitied pre-thoughts or imaginings into one, actual thought. It reduces possibility to actuality.

When we, as it were, open the box and look at Schrödinger's cat, when we make a decision or a choice or concentrate on an idea, we literally create actualities. We pluck one of many possibilities out from the quantum realm and actualize it. In doing so, we are literally acting as midwives to reality.

Through the basic physics of our consciousness, each one

of us stands in relation to the universe as a co-creator, a partner in the unending process of reality's unfolding. We do this at every moment as we take the chaos from our environment and draw it into an ordered whole, whether we are artists or writers or musicians or simply everyday conscious creatures. Creativity is a built-in part of our nature.

NOTES

1. René Descartes, *Meditations,* Indianapolis & New York: Bobbs-Merrill & Co., 1960.
2. Bertrand Russell, "A Free Man's Worship," in *Mysticism and Logic,* New York: Doubleday Anchor, 1957, p. 45.
3. H. Frolich & F. Kremer, eds., *Coherent Excitations in Biological Systems,* Berlin, Heidelberg, New York, & Tokyo: Springer-Verlag, 1983.
4. E. Del Guidice, G. Preparata, & G. Vitiello, "Water as a Free Electric Dipole Laser," *Physical Review Letters,* 61 (1988):1085–1088.
5. H. Fröhlich, "Coherent Excitations in Active Biological Systems," in *Modern Biochemistry,* edited by F. Gutman & H. Keyzer (New York and London: Plenum, 1986).
6. E. Del Guidice et al., "Magnetic Flux Quantization and Josephson Behaviour in Living Systems," *Physica Scripta,* 40 (1989):786–791.
7. Michael P. Stryker, "Is Grandmother an Oscillation?" *Nature,* 338 (23 March 1989), 297–298.
8. I. N. Marshall, "Consciousness and Bose-Einstein Condensates," *New Ideas in Psychology,* 7, no. 1 (1989).
9. Ilya Prigogine and Isabelle Stengers, *Order Out of Chaos,* New York and London: Bantam, 1984.
10. *Ibid.*

CONTRIBUTORS

TERESA M. AMABILE is a psychology professor at Brandeis University who has completed extensive research on the ways that social environments can influence the verbal, artistic, and problem-solving creativity of both children and adults. She is a Fellow of the American Psychological Association and the American Psychological Society and a member of the Board of Trustees of the Creative Education Foundation. She is co-editor of *Psychological Research in the Classroom,* and author of *The Social Psychology of Creativity* and *Growing Up Creative.*

HOWARD GARDNER is Professor of Education at Harvard, co-director of Project Zero, and a longtime neuropsychological researcher at the Boston Veterans Medical Center. Professor Gardner is the recipient of a MacArthur Fellowship and the Grawemeyer Award in Education. He has authored several books in the areas of cognitive psychology, creativity, and the arts.

HOWARD E. GRUBER is Research Scholar of Psychology at Teachers College, Columbia University, and the President of the Division of Psychology and the Arts of the American Psychological Association. He was formerly Professor of Psychology at the University of Geneva and Distinguished Professor at Rutgers University. He is the author of *Darwin on Man: A Psychological Study of Scientific Creativity* (awarded Phi Beta Kappa prize for books in science) as well as the co-editor and author of *Creative People at Work: Twelve Cognitive Case Studies,* and other works concerned both with individual creativity and with its relation to society.

KENNETH HOPE was born in New York City on November 4, 1947. He has a B.S. from the University of Wisconsin (School of Education) and a Ph.D. in comparative literature from Indiana University. He has taught literature, film studies, and writing at the Université de Dijon in France, at Indiana as a Visiting Assistant Professor, at Loyola University in Chicago, and elsewhere. In 1978 he was recruited by Roderick MacArthur to help develop the MacArthur Fellows Program, which he directed from 1982–1992. He is married and has two children.

STUART A. KAUFFMAN is Professor of Biochemistry at the University of Pennsylvania and Maxwell Professor at the Santa Fe Institute for the Study of Complexity. He is editor of the *Journal of Theoretical Biology* and is President of the Society of Mathematical Biology. He is the author of *The Origins of Order,* the first scholarly account of the new science on complexity, to be published by Oxford University Press.

RICHARD MORRIS, theoretical physicist, is author of *Dismantling the Universe, Time's Arrows, The Nature of Reality,* and *The Edges of Science.*

PAT PERRIN is a writer and visual artist living in Portland, Oregon. In collaboration with her husband, Wim Coleman, she has authored a newsletter, a nonfiction book, and a novel, *The Jamais Vu Papers: Misadventures in the Worlds of Science, Myth, and Magic* (Harmony Books, 1991). She and Coleman are currently working on two new novels, *Terminal Games* and *The Madeira Interface: A Cybernetic Romance,* to be published by Bantam in 1993 and 1994.

RICHARD RESTAK, M.D., a neurologist and neuropsychologist, practices medicine in Washington, D.C. He is an Associate Professor of Neurology at the Georgetown University School of Medicine and is the author of nine books about brain and behavior. Articles by Dr. Restak have been published in *Saturday Review*, *Psychology Today*, *The Washington Post*, and *The New York Times*.

DEAN KEITH SIMONTON is Professor of Psychology at the University of California, Davis. He is the author of *Genius, Creativity, and Leadership*, *Why Presidents Succeed*, *Scientific Genius*, and *Psychology, Science, and History*. His next book is *Making a Mark: The Psychology of Big Events and Important People*.

ELIZABETH TIGHE is currently a lecturer in social psychology and research methods in social psychology at Wellesley College and in statistics at Brandeis University. She earned a bachelor's of science in psychology at Carnegie-Mellon University and recently completed her doctorate in social psychology at Brandeis, where she primarily has studied the effects of mood and motivation on creativity.

DANAH ZOHAR is a writer and physicist. Her long career of communicating science ideas to the general public has included several years as a science features writer for the London *Sunday Times*, frequent science book reviews for various British newspapers, and authorship of several books. Her most recent book, *The Quantum Self*, has been sold in the United Kingdom and all of the major European markets.

ABOUT THE EDITOR

JOHN BROCKMAN, president of Edge Foundation and founder of The Reality Club, is a writer and literary agent. His works include *By The Late John Brockman, 37, Afterwards,* and (with Edwin Schlossberg) *The Philosopher's Game, The Pocket Calculator Game Book, The Pocket Calculator Game Book #2, The Kid's Pocket Calculator Game Book, The CB Encyclopedia,* and *The Home Computer Handbook.* He is the editor of *About Bateson,* three Reality Club volumes—*Speculations, Doing Science,* and *Ways of Knowing*—and (with Edward Rosenfeld) *Real Time 1 & 2.*

Mr. Brockman is the publisher and editor of *EDGE,* the newsletter of the Edge Foundation.

He divides his time between New York City and Eastover Farm in Bethlehem, Connecticut.